Daniel Shepardson

The Suffereing Savior

And other sermons. Second Edition

Daniel Shepardson

The Suffereing Savior
And other sermons. Second Edition

ISBN/EAN: 9783337313968

Printed in Europe, USA, Canada, Australia, Japan

Cover: Foto ©Lupo / pixelio.de

More available books at **www.hansebooks.com**

The Suffering Savior
and
Other Sermons

Daniel Shepardson Jr.

The Suffering Savior

and

Other Sermons

BY

Rev. Daniel Shepardson, Jr., Ph.D. (Yale)

(Second Edition—Enlarged and Revised)

Fleming H. Revell Company
Chicago : New York : Toronto
Publishers of Evangelical Literature

Copyright, 1898, by Fleming H. Revell Company

TO MY WIFE

MARY BELLE SMITH,

WHO WAS WILLING TO JOIN HER LIFE TO ONE IN A
WHEEL-CHAIR; WHO FOR FOUR YEARS WITH
RARE SYMPATHY HAS SHARED MY SHADOWS,
AND WHOSE PEACEFUL PRESENCE AND
CONSTANT GOOD CHEER HAVE EN-
HANCED MY SUNSHINE, THESE
PAGES ARE GRATEFULLY
DEDICATED.

CONTENTS

	PAGE
The Suffering Savior	11
The Best Thing in the World	29
Christ, the Motive Power	47
Gradual Growth	62
Working for Jesus	79
The Bible, the Word of God	96
The Dignity and Destiny of Man	112
Sorrows Sanctified	128
Change Your Mind!	145
Two Kinds of Christians	160
Individual Responsibility for Souls	174
Paul's Prayer for the Philippians	192
Thankfulness	199

PREFACE

The following sermons have been used of God in many cities in the Central States, during various seasons of special meetings, while the writer has been traveling about as an Evangelist. They are now published in response to many requests from those who have heard one or more of them, in the hope that they may be a pleasant and profitable souvenir of past experiences, and may render somewhat more permanent the impressions made at the time of their delivery. The frontispiece will remind the reader of the physical background of these thoughts, and it is the fond trust of the writer that some, who are among the "shut-ins," may also derive help and cheer from the perusal of these pages. The religion of Jesus is the only religion that enables us to get along with sorrow and shade without being either discouraged or hardened by them. It alone furnishes the philosopher's stone by which the baser metals, the lead and copper of life, may be changed into the imperishable and invaluable silver and gold of character. All other religions of the world have proved themselves to be religions of despair. They have brought no sweet relief to the burdened heart, and no Balm of Gilead to the broken life. Where other religions have been dismal failures, the religion of Jesus has gloriously triumphed. He does "heal the broken-hearted, preach deliverance to the captives, and set at liberty them that are bruised." Christianity is pre-eminently a religion of joy and sunshine. It brings gladness out of grief, song out of sorrow, sunshine out of shade. It is not a burden, but a boon; not a hindrance, but a help; not a fast or a funeral, but a feast. The call of Christ as of the prophet of old is, "Hearken diligently unto me, and eat ye that which is good, and let your soul delight itself in fatness." That these pages may be blessed by the great Lord of the Harvest to you, and may help you to lead a more cheerful, consecrated, Christian life, is the sincere prayer of the writer

D. S., Jr.

NEWARK, Ohio, July 1, 1898.

PREFACE TO SECOND EDITION

The kind reception given to the first thousand of "The Suffering Savior," and the many evidences of its helpfulness, have led me to enlarge the original collection by adding the last five studies of the present edition. May the Savior continue to make the messages a blessing.

D. S., Jr.

NEWARK, Ohio, Sept. 1, 1899.

The Suffering Savior

Hebrews 2:10.—"*For it became him, for whom are all things and through whom are all things, in bringing many sons unto glory, to make the captain of their salvation perfect through suffering.*"

THE writer of Hebrews in this section of the book is giving us one of the reasons for the sufferings of the Son of God. In the first chapter he has shown us the infinite superiority in nature and office of Jesus Christ to angels. Angels are all declared to be "ministering spirits," like winds or flaming fire, "sent forth to do service for the sake of those that shall inherit salvation." They are the messengers of God, the pages of creation, that flit here and there on the errands of the king, and help to carry out his gracious purposes. They are subordinate beings, lower than God in nature and office, fleeting in appearance and changeable in form. Christ, however, is declared to be "a Son, through whom God made the worlds, upholding all things by the word of his power"; a Son, who, "when he had made purification of sins, sat down on the right hand of the majesty on high," whom God "appointed heir of all things"; a Son, who was the outshining of God's glory, and the very impress of his substance." Of this Christ more excellent things are spoken, even in the Old Testament, than are declared concerning angels. Of Christ God says, in the 2nd psalm, "Thou art my Son, this day have I begotten thee." Again, in another psalm, God says of Christ, "Thy throne, O God, is forever and ever; and the scepter of uprightness is the scepter of thy kingdom. Thou hast loved righteousness and hated iniquity; therefore God, thy God, hath anointed thee with the oil of gladness above thy fellows." And again, "Thou, Lord, in the beginning hast laid the foundation of the earth, and the heavens are the works of thy hands; they shall perish; but thou continuest: and they all shall wax old as doth a garment; and as a mantle shalt thou roll them up, as a garment, and they shall be changed: but thou art the same, and thy years shall not fail." And again, of Christ, God has said in the 110th psalm, "Sit thou on my right hand, until I make thine enemies the footstool of thy feet." Thus Christ is declared to be a most exalted person, high above all angels, and even identified with God. He is Creator, Sustainer, Redeemer, King. He is a Son, is addressed as God, has an everlasting throne, loves righteousness and hates iniquity, has been anointed with the oil of gladness above his fellows, in the beginning laid the foundation of the earth and made the heavens, and at the last will roll them up as a worn-out garment. Earth and heavens shall pass away, or be changed into something new; but he, who preceded them and made them, shall survive the clash of worlds. He, the Christ, shall sit at the right hand of the majesty on high, until all of his foes shall be subdued.

"But," says an objector, "if Christ was Creator, and is Sustainer, Redeemer and ultimate King of all, if he is the outshining of God's glory and the very impress of his substance, if he is God's Son, has an everlasting throne, didst create and will dissolve the worlds; if he is so exalted a person, far above angels, and even identified with God: how did it happen that this same Son, when he was upon earth, appeared to be *inferior* to angels? Angels are immortal. Angels do not partake of flesh and blood, are not susceptible to suffering, nor subject to death. But Christ partook of flesh and blood, was a man among men, lived a life of hardship and suffering, and died a death of shame. How will you account for these sufferings of Jesus? Were they not inconsistent with his divine position and prerogative?" It is in his answer to this objection that the writer of the book of Hebrews gives us the words of our text, "For it became him, for whom are all things, and through whom are all things, in bringing many sons unto glory, to make the captain of their salvation perfect through suffering." "It became him," it seemed fitting to God, it commended itself to him; to him "for whom are all things, and through whom are all things," to him who had all power and all resources, and before whom were all possible plans of salvation; it seemed good to him in the process of "bringing many sons to glory"—he wanted more sons like Jesus Christ, and his object was to bring these sons to glory—it seemed good to him "to make the captain (or author) of their salvation perfect through suffering"; not perfect in the sense of being made free from fault or flaw, free from sin, for Christ was absolutely and always sinless; but perfect in the sense of having been thus perfectly fitted to do his work as a sympathizing Savior, and as High Priest for humanity. In other words, to God, who had boundless resources, the path of suffering seemed to commend itself as the best possible way by which Christ should become fully fitted to be the captain of salvation for a sinful and suffering world. This verse, then, brings strikingly before our minds the thought of fellow-suffering as the real basis of sympathy, and sympathy as the true basis of helpfulness, about which I wish now to say a few things.

1. Fellow-suffering is the longest line of sympathy. Blood-relationship is usually a basis

of sympathy. People born of common parents generally have a fellow-feeling one for another, have an interest in and sympathy for each other. Brother sympathizes with brother, and relative with relative. The basis of this sympathy is this blood-relationship, but this is a very short line and small circle of sympathy, embracing only a few individuals at the most. Again, persons of the same circle in society, of kindred tastes, of similar professions or occupations, or of similar religious persuasion, have a mutual interest in and sympathy for each other. Doctors are interested in doctors, lawyers in lawyers, etc. This is a sympathy based upon social, professional or religious relationship, and is a still longer line of sympathy than that of family ties, embracing a much larger circle of people. Again, people born in the same city or state, or who are citizens of the same great nation, usually have a fellow-feeling for one another, have sympathy with each other. This fellow-feeling, based upon civic or national lines, may not always be so very prominent in one's thinking, but may lie dormant until some unusual occasion calls it into action. For instance, what a burst of manifested patriotism has been suddenly called forth by our war with Spain! What a national fellow-feeling has been aroused into consciousness by these stirring events, until you and I, every one of us, has the keenest, liveliest interest in everything that concerns the welfare of every "boy in blue," whether he assists in reconstructing government in nearby Cuba, or in establishing and maintaining peace and order in the far-away Philippines! National relationship, patriotism, love of a common country, is the basis of this fellow-feeling; it is a long line of sympathy, embracing seventy millions of people. But there is yet a still longer line of sympathy, based not upon family ties, nor upon social, professional, or religious relationship, nor upon civic or national kinship, but based upon fellow-suffering. Ever since sin entered the world by man's voluntary transgression, one lot has been the common experience of all members of the race. We are all of us sinners, and all of us sufferers. The world is full of sin and filled with suffering; and because this is so, suffering makes the whole world kin. Even the suffering Cubans, though foreigners in language, customs and race, became our fellows, aroused our sympathies, and plunged a great nation into a costly and bloody war, for suffering is the longest line of sympathy. And so when the great God, yearning over fallen and falling men, determined to send his own Son to be the captain of their salvation, in order that the Christ might be most intimately and closely related to every member of a suffering race, in order that the Christ might get a strong hold upon men, it seemed good to him, "for whom are all things, and through whom are all things, in bringing many sons to glory, to make the captain of their salvation perfect through suffering." Had Christ lived among men as an earthly king, surrounded with all the pomp and pride of power and separated from suffering and want, it would doubtless have seemed more in accord with divine position and prerogative, but he would not in that case have been the Christ for you and for me. Far off from our wants and woes, with no sufferings or sorrows or trials, he would not have had real fellow-feeling or sympathy with us, and without sympathy with us, he could not help us; for fellow-suffering is the true basis of sympathy, and sympathy is the real basis of helpfulness. Had Christ lived in the so-called middle class of society, experiencing its comforts and trials, he would have been able to sympathize with and help them, and all more favored than they; but he would hardly have been able to help those who were at the bottom of the social ladder, whose sufferings and trials were so numerous and so heavy. But, when the great Son of God, Creator, Sustainer, Redeemer, King; when he who was the outshining of God's glory, and the very impress of his substance; when he who made and will dissolve the worlds, he who shall sit at God's right hand, until his enemies shall be made the footstool of his feet; when he was born into our suffering world, of humble and poor parentage, taking upon himself the form of a servant, living a life of suffering and dying a death of shame, "borrowing a cradle from the cattle, and a grave from a friend"; then God's love and God's wisdom were manifested in making the captain of our salvation perfect through suffering.

2. Again, note that suffering, like joy, is limited by capacity. Some people have more capacity for sorrow or joy than other people. Some persons live a sort of negative, passive existence, on a dead level, like a plain, with few mountain peaks of exaltation and lofty joy, and few valleys of depression or deep pain. Some people suffer less than others, because of having less capacity for suffering. Others have a large, full, receptive nature, capable of rarest, purest delight, and also capable of deepest, darkest trial and suffering. And so when we think of "The Suffering Savior," we must keep in mind the largeness of his capacity. Capacity, both for sorrow and joy, was at its maximum in Christ. He was in the largest and fullest sense *a man*, every inch a man, pre-eminently the Son of Man. No one else on earth could know the height and purity of his joy, for no one else had such a capacity for gladness; no one else on earth could know the depth and awfulness of his dark sorrows, for no one else had such a finely strung and sensitive soul. You and I will never experience down here the highest altitudes of "the joy of the Lord," because we have not yet the capacity to receive them; nor

will you and I *ever* (for there'll be no sorrow there) be called to pass through shadows and sorrows as deep as those which he experienced, because our souls, with their limited capacities, cannot fathom such depths. Our joys, compared with his joys, are like starlight compared with the glow of the noontide sun; our trials and sorrows are unto his trials and sorrows as twilight shades to midnight gloom. And then, too, when we think of "The Suffering Savior," we must not minimize the reality of his manhood. Christ was a real man. There seems to be a tendency in human thinking to swing like a pendulum from one extreme to the other on this subject. Sometimes men make so much of the divinity of Christ as to forget his humanity. Sometimes men make so much of his humanity as to forget his divinity. Some men find it hard to accept in their thinking the Christ of the Gospels, who is really God, and yet truly man. Some men find it hard to take the Christ as the Bible-writers and history found him. One of the great arguments for the faithfulness and trustworthiness of the Gospel narrators is that they record the facts both of his divinity and of his humanity, without any attempt to explain or reconcile them. His humanity and his divinity were both of them real and genuine, and were often manifested side by side in a very striking way.* For instance,

---

* *Cf.* Stalker's "Trial and Death of Jesus Christ."

Christ, after a hard day's work of teaching and healing in Capernaum, desires quiet and rest, and asks the disciples to get a boat and push out upon the lake. The disciples do so, and Christ lies down, tired and weary, upon a pillow in the stern of the boat. Soon he is fast asleep, so soundly asleep as not to be disturbed by the tossing of the boat, or by the storm that is now raging; so soundly asleep that it was necessary roughly to shake him, in order to arouse him. It is the deep sleep of a weary man. But now, as the disciples wake him with the troubled cry, "Master, carest thou not that we perish?" Christ arises from his sleep, rebukes the storm, and commands the troubled elements, "Peace, be still." "And there was a great calm." The disciples were amazed, and doubtless felt, "It's the voice of God!" Again, we see this Christ at the tomb of a friend, and amid the grief and sadness of the scene, "Jesus wept." They are the tears of a man. And then, in a few moments, we hear him as he stands before the rock tomb of his dead friend and cries, "Lazarus, come forth"; and, at the call of God, the dead awakes. Ah, yes! he was both God and man; and you and I will lose much of the sweet helpfulness of the Christ of the Gospels, if we minimize in our thinking either his divinity or his humanity. In thinking, then, of Christ, the Sufferer, remember at all times the reality of his humanity. Bear in mind that he

THE SUFFERING SAVIOR

had a human body, that he was born of a woman, that he grew in wisdom and stature as other men, that he was hungry and thirsty and weary, feeling the same kind of hunger and thirst and weariness that you and I feel. Bear in mind that he needed rest and sleep, that he was susceptible to physical suffering and pain, that he "sweat, as it were, great drops of blood falling down to the ground," that he fainted beneath the cross, was scourged and crucified, died and was buried. Bear in mind that he had a rational nature, that he was subject to temptation, that he had emotions of joy and grief, that he felt compassion and had displeasure, that he needed and practiced prayer. Above all things, remember his sorrows and his troubles. Indeed, "he was a man of sorrows and acquainted with grief"; he had sorrows in his own life, and was familiar with the woes of others: grief, from the bereavement of death; grief, from the unfaithfulness of his dearest friends; grief, from the treachery of one who sat at meat with him; grief, from the vicious and unrelenting hate which followed him everywhere from those who should have been his friends; grief, from seeing the wickedness of the wicked, and knowing the certainty of their doom; grief, from realizing his helplessness to save those who would not come to him that they might be saved. Ah! surely, he was the "man of sorrows and acquainted with grief"; surely, the captain of our salvation was made "perfect through suffering!"

And yet, though perfectly fitted to be our sympathizing Savior, many live and die without the abiding consciousness of his helpfulness. Some months ago, in a neighboring city, a burdened one opened her heart to me and told me her sorrow. She was a hunchback girl, and felt lonely and hungry for companionship. "You know," she said, to the man in the wheel-chair, "my heart aches; I'm so lonely! I tell you this because I feel sure that you, in your physical condition, will understand my meaning. There are times when Jesus don't seem to help me any, and they too are the times when I need him the most. You know. I get so lonely! I feel so much alone in the world! The hunch on my back separates me from everybody else; even my own mother don't understand me. No one knows my peculiar trials and troubles. I am, at times, so much alone! Even Jesus is not company for me." And then, in order still further to draw her out, I said, "How is it that Jesus can't help you?" "Ah," said she, "Jesus didn't have any hunch on his back, did he? He never knew how it felt to be so lonesome!" Then I began to tell to her again the story of Jesus. I told her of his glory with the Father before the worlds were. I told her of the purity and sweet companionship of heaven, of the society of the angels, of how

Jesus so loved us that he left all of these things and came down to earth to die for us. I told her how coldly he was received; how, when he made known in his home town his friendly and merciful mission, his fellow citizens took him out to the edge of a precipice and wished to hurl him headlong to destruction. I told her of his rejection by Capernaum and Gadara, by Samaria and Judea; how "he came unto his own and his own received him not"; how he wept over Jerusalem because of her hard-heartedness; how he was misunderstood by friend and foe; how he could not make known the deepest thoughts of his heart, because the people of earth were not able to receive them; how even his disciples had constantly materialistic and selfish thoughts, while he was speaking to them of spiritual things. I told her of the far remove between his sinless soul and the best thoughts of earth's purest ones. I pictured forth his natural sociability and his lack of congenial companions, his loneliness when he cried, "The foxes have holes and the birds of the air have nests, but the Son of Man hath not where to lay his head"; for humanity had shut its doors and its hearts against him. And then I told her of Gethsemane and those trying hours; how he took the eleven with him into the garden (one of his twelve most intimate followers was even now selling him for thirty pieces of silver). I told her how he longed to have friends near him in the hours of struggle; how, feeling perhaps their lack of sympathy, he left the eleven and taking the three, Peter, James and John, went still further into the Garden; how, leaving even the three, he went alone into the deeper gloom, and fell headlong on the ground and agonized. The loneliness and struggle of those hours, who can picture! And then he returned to his friends for sympathy and help. Were they watching and sharing his sorrow? Ah, no; they were fast asleep. He was alone in his trouble. And then I told her of his arrest, and how all forsook him and fled. I told her of his trial and scourging and cruel mocking; and how, when he hung upon the cross, the gloom seemed so dark that even the face of God seemed to be hidden from him, and he cried out in his loneliness and woe, "My God! my God! why hast thou forsaken me?" Then, turning to the hunchback girl, I said, "Do you think you ever felt as lonesome as Jesus did? Don't you think that he can sympathize with and help you now?" "Yes," she said, "I see it now, and I will accept him as my sympathizing Savior in every sorrow." "For it became him, for whom are all things, and through whom are all things, in bringing many sons unto glory, to make the captain of their salvation perfect through suffering."

Again, we must remember that this sympathizing Jesus is just the same to-day as of old. When he ascended on high, he did not lay aside his humanity, his capacity for sympathy, his human fellow-feeling; for the Christ who sits to-day on the right hand of the majesty on high is the glorified God-Man, Christ Jesus. His perfect humanity has been crowned and glorified, but not given up. He is still "Jesus Christ, the same yesterday, to-day and forever." "In him dwelleth all the fulness of the Godhead bodily." We still "have a great high priest who hath passed through the heavens"; "not a high priest that cannot be touched with the feeling of our infirmities, but one who was in all points tempted like as we are." "For in that he himself hath suffered being tempted, he is able to succor them that are tempted." The Christ in heaven is yet "a lamb as it had been slain." In his exaltation he does not forget the experiences of his humiliation. He is now "the captain of our salvation perfect through suffering."

3. It follows, then, from these considerations, that the reason why many have rejected Christ is just the reason why they should accept him. The Jews rejected Christ because of the lowliness of his life, because he refused to live as kings usually live. A royal Messiah they were ready to crown, but a suffering Messiah they hasted to crucify. Had Jesus on Palm Sunday come into Jerusalem on a charging war-horse and as a military conqueror, the result would doubtless have been

different from what it was, when he came into Jerusalem upon a humble beast of burden, and as the Prince of Peace. The man of sorrows was not to the Jews' liking, although it was through those very sorrows that he was perfectly fitted to meet their need. Paul found that a crucified Christ was "to the Jews a stumbling-block, and to the Greeks foolishness"; and yet, after all, he was "the power of God and the wisdom of God unto salvation" to all who believe; for it seemed best "to him, for whom are all things, and through whom are all things, in bringing many sons to glory, to make the captain of their salvation perfect through suffering." Moreover, to-day there are some who reject the divine Christ because of his human sufferings; and yet these very sufferings were endured that he might the more fully identify himself with those whom he came to save, and by sympathizing with them help them.

4. And now, in conclusion, let us note that as Christ through his sufferings became the better fitted to be our sympathizing and helpful Savior, so we, through our sufferings, may become the better fitted to be helpful to our suffering fellows. It is only those, who themselves have really suffered, who can have the truest and deepest sympathy with those who suffer. This is one of the most precious of the many compensations which come to the sufferer that—in addition to the

lessons of patience and faith which it is his high privilege to learn; in addition to the deeper appreciation of the sufferings, sympathy, companionship and promises of the Savior, which it is his blessed lot to have; in addition to the purifying and strengthening of his own character, which the submissive, cheerful and Christian endurance of trials and suffering always brings about—in addition to all these blessings, he who suffers may gain, if he will, from his own sufferings an enlarged capacity for sympathy with and helpfulness to others. What a privilege it is for the suffering ones of earth, by living cheerful, courageous lives in the midst of many shadows, to be able to cheer, comfort and help others in their trials! This thought was evidently in the mind of Paul, that happy, thankful Christian of many perils and much suffering, when he exclaimed in the opening chapter of his second letter to the Corinthians: "Blessed be God, even the Father of our Lord Jesus Christ, the Father of mercies, and the God of all comfort; who comforteth us in all our tribulation, that we may be able to comfort them which are in any trouble, by the comfort wherewith we ourselves are comforted of God." And so, O burdened one, do not be cast down by your trials, but find refuge in the Captain of your salvation, who was made perfect through suffering; and let not your sorrows and suffering harden you, but rather may they increase your capacity for sympathy and helpfulness, and send you out to cheer and comfort others with the comfort wherewith you yourself have been comforted of God.

The Best Thing in the World

✣ ✣ ✣

Matt. 13:44-46.—"*The kingdom of heaven is like unto a treasure hidden in the field; which a man found, and hid; and in his joy he goeth and selleth all that he hath, and buyeth that field. Again, the kingdom of heaven is like unto a man that is a merchant seeking goodly pearls: and having found one pearl of great price, he went and sold all that he had, and bought it.*"

✣ ✣ ✣

AS one passes along a thoroughfare of any of our cities, and notices the people with eager faces thronging hither and thither, the question often arises, "What is it that each one is seeking so earnestly? What is that thing of such high value as to be worthy of such a relentless pursuit?" Some are seeking pleasure, some wealth, some wisdom, some power. All of them are in pursuit, directly or indirectly, of something which they regard as a good thing, the winning of which would result in personal gain. But the ends at which they are aiming are so various, and differ so much in actual value. Some are high, some are low, some are of great worth, some are valueless; and the old question recurs again and again, "What is the best thing in the world?" What is that thing supremely desirable, for the attainment of which it were well, if necessary, to lose all things else? What is the chief good, the *summum bonum*, as the ancients called it? Is there, after all, some one thing which, for all people, irrespective of age, sex or condition, is of highest value? If so, what is it, and how can we obtain it?

1. Various answers have been given to this first question, "What is the chief good?" These answers have differed one from another as the answers to a corresponding question have been different. That probably is the greatest good for each one of us which will hinder and destroy that which causes us the most harm. Tell me what you regard as the greatest evil of existence, and I can readily determine what you think to be the greatest good. Let us recall some of the things that have been and are regarded by men as of supreme worth.

It is thought by many that the greatest evil of existence is physical evil. That sickness and suffering, bodily disease and decay are the essence of human ills. Corresponding with this view of evil is the view that physical health is the greatest blessing which any individual can possess. To be sound in body, and to remain so, is to have the chief good. Led on by this idea, Ponce de Leon, an old man, rich but weakened with age, set out on the 27th of March, 1513, from Porto Rico, with three caravels to cross again the wide Atlantic, in search of the longed for "Fountain of Perpetual Youth," which Spanish folk-lore said was situated in the islands beyond the sea. When, after days of westward sailing, they sighted the southeastern shore of our continent, at that time green and beautiful to the water's edge, their enthusiasm rose to the highest pitch, and in their delight they named the place "Florida," "the land of flowers." Surely, such a bower of bloom and beauty could only be fertilized by a fountain of perpetual youth. Surely, in such a haven health and strength would be permanent. You recall how expectantly Ponce de Leon and his men explored the woods and searched the valleys, hopefully bathing in every stream and eagerly drinking of every spring, in search of the waters of immortality. But, alas! they were never found. De Leon returned to Porto Rico, a broken-down and disappointed man, only to die of wounds received on his fruitless journey. Health of body, freedom from pain, must always be indeed a great boon. Farthest is it from my thoughts to underestimate its real worth. It is a gift of God to be devoutly grateful for, to be guarded with zealous care. But it is not the supreme good. There is something of higher value than this. It is possible for one to enjoy for many years practically perfect health, and yet miss entirely the supreme good. There is something better, to gain which it were profitable, if necessary, even to lose this so-called chief good.

In other days there were those who openly avowed that the greatest good is pleasure, whose motto was, "Let us eat, drink and be merry, for to-morrow we die"—Epicureans, who thought the greatest good in life was just to have a good time. Even in this age of Christian civilization and enlightenment there seem to be many followers of this ancient, heathen philosophy. But it has always been true, that those who have sought happiness in itself as the chief good, have always ended by being themselves most miserable; having found that this, which was supposed to be the chief good, was in truth but a deceptive dream. The writer of Ecclesiastes presents to us one who gave himself up unreservedly to having a good time, and who drank to the full of every pleasure possible, even to a king of limitless resources and unbridled appetites; but at the end of his full round of pleasure, when he had tasted all of her sweets, he sadly but wisely wrote, "Vanity of vanities, vanity of vanities, all is vanity." It is also worthy of note that the so-called "school of pleasure" never yet has produced a really great man.

THE BEST THING IN THE WORLD

Again, men have said that the greatest of all ills is financial distress; that poverty is the mainspring of human woe, and that, correspondingly, the greatest good is money, wealth. This seems to be the prevailing idea in the minds of many Americans to-day. We are said to worship the "Almighty Dollar." This we believe to be a libel upon the American people. But we see also much ground for the accusation in the eagerness to amass fortunes and in the materialistic direction taken by so much of our endeavor. Wealth, however, cannot be the greatest boon, for in many cases it proves to be the greatest of curses, and those who have the most of it seldom regard themselves as most fortunate. Xerxes, with all of his wealth of armies, fleets and countless gold, was far from happy, and offered a prize to the inventor of some new pleasure. Men in all ages have sought to find the chief good in wealth, only to be disappointed. And one, whose authority has never been questioned, has said, "What shall it profit a man, if he gain the whole world and lose his own soul?" And of another, who had amassed great wealth and felt that he had the greatest good, it was said, "Thou fool! this night shall thy soul be required of thee; then whose shall those things be which thou hast provided? So is he that layeth up treasure for himself, and is not rich toward God."

Again, it has been said that power, or conquest,

is the greatest good. We have seen an Alexander, driven by this thought, sweep over a whole world with restless might, conquering everything before him. And yet, when he had been uniformly successful and was without a foe resisting, we are told that he "sat down and wept because there were no more worlds to conquer." Surely, that which is of highest worth, when won, should be all-satisfying.

Others have said that ignorance is the cause of the greatest evil, and that knowledge must, consequently, be the greatest good. In all ages of the world there have been those of higher perception who have felt that knowledge is the greatest of all boons. The student spends years of hardest toil in pursuit of this great good. Men and women of great perseverance and faith have spent a lifetime of active research in the attempt to add something to the volume of knowledge. Surely, this is a noble aim; this is a lofty conception of life. But knowledge in itself cannot be the supreme good in life. I recall that Socrates prayed: "O, Pan, make me to know that he is rich who is wise"; and, though this must ever be regarded as a very high ideal, yet there was a greater teacher than Socrates in view of whose teachings even this high conception must be regarded as falling short of the highest. Thus we have seen a few of the answers that have been given to the question, "What is the chief good?"

Is it health? Is it pleasure? Is it wealth? Is it power? Is it knowledge? Men have answered the question so differently. Is it a question, after all, of real importance?

2. A radical difference between man and the lower animals is that lower animals always act by instinct, while the acts of man are put forth in view of a rational choice. The horse eats, sleeps, and spends its time in various ways, not in view of any ultimate end at which it has arrived by a course of reasoning, but impelled by the inborn laws of its own existence which we call instinct. It does not live according to any plan, or in view of any final purpose. Man, however, is a reasoning animal, and acts in view of certain ends to be attained. True it is that some, whom by courtesy we call men, do not seem to have any aim in existence, and do not live under the impulse of any end to be attained, people who seem to drift here and there as the tide ebbs or flows. But even they, in the final analysis, are seen to act always, consciously or unconsciously, in view of certain ends to be attained. It may be, indeed, a very ignoble one, as the gambler's aim, to get as much as possible for nothing; or the tramp's, to do as little work as possible. Or man's final purpose, in conscious or unconscious view of which all of his acts are put forth, may be a noble impulse, which drives him on with terrible zeal, and will

not let him rest, until the end desired has been achieved.

Now, the determining of the question, "What is the best thing in life?" will have a very decided influence in determining what the final purpose of one's life shall be. Moreover, whatever becomes the final purpose of one's life will become the determining factor in all of one's thoughts, feelings and actions. It will determine the employment of one's time; will give direction to one's endeavors; will mould one's habits and determine one's character; and character here will determine destiny hereafter. As some one has so truly said:

> "Sow a thought, you reap a deed;
> Sow a deed, you reap a habit;
> Sow a habit, you reap a character;
> Sow a character, you reap a destiny."

The determining, then, of what is the best thing in the world is the settlement of a question of supreme importance, a question of far-reaching results, a question which determines character and destiny.

Sad would it be for us, if we were left in such an important matter to the conflicting opinions of men simply, men who have differed so widely as to what is of supreme worth. Fortunate indeed are we that we have a higher court, a court of ultimate appeal, a tribunal whose authority.

trustworthiness and honor have never been impeached, a teacher of whom even his enemies said, "No man ever so spake."

In view, then, of the conflicting opinions of men, in view of the supreme importance of the question, we refer it for final solution to the great teacher come from God, the Christ of Nazareth.

3. To the unerring mind of Christ, to him who was the light of the world, to him who was the way, the truth and the life, all things appeared as they really are. He alone saw with undimmed vision, and declared the fact, that the greatest evil of existence is not physical evil, not poverty of pocket, limitation of power, or ignorance of mind, but domination of self and selfishness; that the great sickness of the world, and of each individual in it, is sin, which is the expression of selfishness; that the great need of each individual is to be freed from the dominion of self and sin. Accordingly, he came not as the deliverer from the dominion of Rome, for that was not the great need. He came to deliver mankind from themselves. In accord, then, with the chief purpose of his divine mission, in two of his parables Christ set forth the truth concerning what was of supreme worth. He taught that the chief good, the thing to be won, even at the loss of all things else, if necessary, the thing of supreme value to every person, irrespective of age, sex or condition, the thing worthy of supreme regard, was the

kingdom of heaven; not referring in these sayings to the kingdom of heaven as an external, visible society, as that reign of equity and peace which shall ultimately subdue the world and usher in a new order of things, a new heaven and a new earth in which dwelleth righteousness; not having in mind, I take it, this aspect of the kingdom of heaven so much as the idea of the kingdom of heaven as an internal, individual possession, the kingdom of heaven within every man's heart, the result of Christ's purifying and peace-giving presence.* This kingdom of heaven, as an individual possession, is the greatest individual good; this is the thing of supreme value. Christ said, "The kingdom of heaven is like unto a treasure hidden in the field; which a man found and hid, and in his joy he goeth and selleth all that he hath, and buyeth that field." And, again, in calling attention to the superlative value of the kingdom, he said, "Again, the kingdom of heaven is like unto a merchant seeking goodly pearls: and having found one pearl of great price, he went and sold all that he had, and bought it." Not only in these two parables, but in other striking teachings of the Savior the same truth is emphasized. "Seek ye first the kingdom of God and his righteousness." Why first? First in time

---

*In this Sermon and in "Gradual Growth" the author desires to express his great obligations to the writings of Prof. A. B. Bruce.

and first in importance, because it is of supreme worth. Again, he said, "Let the dead bury their dead, but go thou and preach the kingdom of God," i. e., even the most sacred rites and ceremonies are to be held in less esteem than the kingdom of God. It alone is of supreme value. "No man having put his hand to the plow and looking back is fit for the kingdom of God." It deserves undivided allegiance, and should be held in highest regard. And again, "He that loveth father or mother more than me is not worthy of me; and he that loveth son or daughter more than me is not worthy of me." Christ and his kingdom alone are worthy of the highest place. There can be no doubt, then, from these parables and sayings, as to the mind of the Master regarding the chief good.

Let us note, in passing, to what in these two parables our Master likens this chief good. In the first parable it is likened unto a treasure hid in a field, and in the second to a pearl of great price. Both of these comparisons are, at first thought, rather surprising. Why liken this greatest of all blessings to a treasure hid in a field? Is there, then, no more probability of one obtaining it than of one finding a hid treasure? Then, indeed, most of us would best give up the quest at once And why compare this greatest good to so common a jewel as a pearl? Surely the diamond, the largest of diamonds, rather than a pearl of great price, would be a more appropriate parallel. But in both of these queries we have lost sight of a very important consideration which must always be kept in view when interpreting the Bible. While the Bible, under the far-reaching providence of God, was intended as a book for all times and all places, and as a revelation of God's will to all peoples in every age of the world, yet it arose out of historical situations. Its peculiar forms of thought and illustration were moulded with reference, primarily, to the forceful teaching of the original hearers and readers. And we must remember that while it is the Bible for the world, it is also peculiarly oriental, and has the ear-marks of the ages which form its background. Christ was speaking to an oriental audience in the first century of this era. The hiding of treasure in a field, or in the caverns of the hill-side, in that time and place of frequent robberies, when banks, safety deposit vaults and sure investments were not known, was a very common way of concealing valuables, and the chance finding of such hidden treasure was also a common occurrence. And the fact of the treasure being hid is but an evidence of its value as being worth hiding. Again, the diamond, which, in our day, is the usual symbol of priceless value, was, in the times of Christ, comparatively unknown, and the pearl occupied as a symbol of value a similar place in the oriental mind to the

THE BEST THING IN THE WORLD 41

diamond in ours. You recall that the lavish display of wealth made by Cleopatra reached its culmination in pearls of magnificent worth, some of which were estimated at a value equal to $500,000 of our money. When she wished to manifest her reckless devotion to Antony, it was priceless pearls that were so rashly sacrificed. Had Christ in his day compared the supreme worth of the kingdom of heaven to the worth of a priceless diamond, he would have used an illustration wholly beyond the comprehension of his hearers, the common people. There is, then, no doubt as to the teaching of Christ concerning the greatest good. The thing of supreme worth to every individual is the kingdom of heaven as an individual possession, the result of the purifying and peace-giving presence of Jesus in the believer's soul. Not health of body, not pleasure, not wealth, not power, not knowledge even; none of these things is the chief good, but the kingdom of God incarnated in the individual. This is the one thing of supreme worth, the one thing of highest value to every person, irrespective of age, sex or condition.

4. This is the chief good, but many do not so regard it. In the parables of the Sower and of the Great Supper, Christ clearly set forth the attitude of many toward the kingdom. Some, the wayside hearers, are entirely indifferent to its worth. Some, the stony ground hearers,

impulsively seize upon it; but their emotion, supported by no depth of conviction, does not long continue, and the chief good soon disappears from view. Others, the thorny ground hearers, take it into their lives, but fail to recognize that it must have supreme and absolute control; other things are given a greater or less degree of allegiance, and, sooner or later, these other and antagonistic things dethrone the chief good and drive it out from any practical control of the life. But others there are, the good ground hearers, who regard the kingdom as the one supreme thing, the one thing of superlative worth, deserving of highest place and absolute loyalty. These make Christian character the one end of life, and they alone succeed in making the kingdom truly their own. Again, in the parable of the Great Supper, the Master taught how men are continually putting other things less worthy in the place of the chief good. This chief good is represented as a great feast and many are invited. But one regards the land which he has recently purchased of more importance; a second one considers his yoke of oxen more valuable; while a third much prefers the company of his newly married wife. All of these things were good in themselves, but the feast should have been the thing of supreme moment. And to-day there are many people absorbed in things that in themselves are all right, but which, when they take

THE BEST THING IN THE WORLD 43

the place that belongs to the chief good, become a curse instead of a blessing. One of the most important lessons of life is to learn to keep things in their proper place, to put that first which ought to be first, and never to let that which is of secondary importance get our primary allegiance. And we need so to live and to learn and to pray, that we may have an undimmed vision of that which is of highest value, and that we may keep that thing of highest worth as our one chief aim.

5. The true attitude of every man toward this greatest good is taught by Christ in the parables read at the beginning of the hour. The man who found the hidden treasure and perceived that this was the most valuable thing, gladly went and sold all that he had and bought the field; while he that found the pearl of great price disposed of all his other pearls in order to obtain this one, which he saw was better than all others. This is the attitude demanded of all who would make this kingdom their own. The promise is, "Ye shall seek me and ye shall find me, when ye search for me with all your heart." The answer given to the rich young man, who worshiped his wealth and who desired to know what he must do to inherit the kingdom, was, "Go, sell all that thou hast and give to the poor, and thou shalt have treasure in heaven." Whatever stands in the way must be sacrificed. Other idols must be dethroned. This is the price which must be paid

for the kingdom. A large factor in determining the worth of an article is the cost of production, and this highest good, Christian character, is the most costly of all products. It cost the Son of God an infinite price, paid with his own precious blood, that it might become possible for us. It will cost us a lifetime of self-denial and devotion before we make it fully our own. Let no one suppose that this in any way contradicts the freedom of God's offer of salvation. We are saved by grace; it is the gift of God; not of works, lest any man should glory; and yet we are urged to work out our own salvation with fear and trembling; for it is God that worketh in us both to will and to do of his good pleasure. We are freely made sons of God through faith in Christ; but we need also to grow in grace and in the knowledge of his will, and to strive to attain to the fullness of the stature of men and women in Christ. If we are to attain to full Christian manhood, we need to put the kingdom first. We need to be willing to sacrifice all other things to this one supreme end. We need to put out of our lives all things which hinder, in any way, the winning in the fullest sense this supreme good. We need to subordinate and bring under the demands of Christian character all other pursuits, the acquisition of wealth, the pursuit of pleasure, the winning of fame, or the getting of knowledge. We must first be Christians, then learned lawyers, successful doctors, wealthy merchants and honored workers in other lines as calling and industry may permit. What the church and the world need to-day above all things else is men and women who will put Christian character first. To-day the striking spectacle is witnessed of thousands of men seeking places, and thousands of places seeking men. There are plenty of places and plenty of applicants; but there are so few men and women. Over the door of every profession and vocation in life there has always been a standing advertisement: "Wanted, Men." Not dwarfs, not pigmies, not lopsided freaks; but well-developed, symmetrical men. Men with large hearts as well as heads, trained to feel and to act as well as to think. Men who are larger than their professions, who care more for character than reputation, more for integrity than honor, more for manhood than money. Whatever, then, is your profession or occupation in life, be it to handle "plow or plane, the pick or the pen," be it humble or high, prominent or obscure, whatever your occupation, make Christian manhood your business. Be willing, in seeking this highest good, to act as men in other lines act, when they are pursuing what they falsely suppose to be of highest worth. Let us give ourselves unreservedly to it. Let us make it the passion of our lives. Pursue it with unflagging zeal. Give it the devotion of a Nathan Hale, who nobly said, "I regret that I have but one life to give to my country." Pursue it with the perseverance of a Paul, who said, "This one thing I do, forgetting the things which are behind, and reaching forth unto those things which are before, I press toward the mark for the prize of the high calling of God in Christ Jesus!" If, then, we make Christian character the chief end of life, and pursue it with the diligence and devotion that it deserves, the days spent here will be a joy and a blessing to ourselves and to others; and over yonder there will be a larger and fuller development of the life which here was only begun.

> "Wanted Men!
> Not systems fit and wise;
> Not faiths with rigid eyes;
> Not wealth in mountain piles;
> Not power with gracious smiles;
> Not even the potent pen;
>   Wanted Men!"

Christ the Motive Power

2 Cor. 5:14.—*"For the love of Christ constraineth us"* (*impels us, drives us on*).

ONE of the most interesting and far-reaching questions in the wide-awake, scientific world of to-day is the question of motive power. What force, what power is best adapted to turn the wheels of manufacture, to whirl our trains across the continent, to speed our ships over the seas and to drive our cars through the streets of our rapidly growing cities? What force is to furnish the enginery of civilization? This is now the great question in the scientific world.

Likewise, in the moral world as well as in the physical world, the great question from the beginning of time has been the question of motive power. What force, what power is sufficient to reach down and take hold of weak, selfish, sin-cursed men and women, living in the malarial swamps of evil, and lift them up to a higher, purer plane of life? What force is sufficient to enable man to break the bonds of self and to get free from the toils of sin?

Various systems of philosophy and religion have been offered as a cure for the ills of sin, and as a sufficient inspiration to a higher, better life. The main difference between them has been a difference of motive power, and their failure or partial success has been due to the inefficiency or the partial sufficiency of the motive power provided. In the far-reaching providence of God, these systems have been allowed or inspired to prove their own insufficiency, and to prepare the way for the only religion which ever has been offered, or would be offered with a motive power adequate for the purpose. Three great nations of antiquity preceded the coming of Christ, and each in its own, or rather in God's own way, prepared the way for his coming. Each of them offered a motive power to a higher life, which proved defective, and which only made more manifest to the world the world's need of something better. Consider, then, with me this morning three huge failures and one magnificent success:

THREE HUGE FAILURES

1. Greece: The God of Greece was culture. The Greeks tried to furnish in the cultivation of the intellect a motive power sufficiently strong to uplift and save man. The sense of "the noble, the beautiful and the true," aroused in man, was to restrain him from the shame, ugliness and

falsity of sin. Proper perception of the real worth of things would be a motive sufficient to lead a man to choose the better and to reject the worse. But should the question arise, "How arouse this saving sense of 'the noble, the beautiful and the true'?" how give men a proper perception of the real worth of things? The answer the Greek gave was, "By education." The highest representative of this idea was Socrates, who through his pupil, Plato, has given us a most profound attempt to uplift and save the race.

Plato believed in a personal, self-conscious, supreme Being, a God; but a God afar off, entirely beyond the ken of man, surrounded with mystery and himself unknowable. But side by side with this far-off, unknowable God was a world of patterns, models, divine ideals, according to which all visible things in this material world of ours are formed, and of which models the visible world is but an imperfect copy. Now and then, Plato believed, there is a man of acute mental perception, of keen spiritual insight, a philosopher perhaps, who is caught up to a third heaven, as it were, upon the wings of inspiration, and from this mountain top is given a sight, a vision of these patterns, models, forms of the divine mind, of which our world is the imperfect copy. This beatific vision would be forever afterwards an inspiration to draw him to higher things. This was a beautiful conception of Plato's, but alas! it had two serious defects. This vision at best lasted but a moment, and was not long enough continued, nor oft enough repeated to prove a lifetime inspiration. And then, too, only those of keenest intellect could have this vision. No provision was made for the salvation of the average man. Only a very few at the most could ever be saved. And so the best that Greece, the best that culture, could do, failed to change the life, to restrain from sin, or to renew the heart.

2. Rome: The God of Rome was law. The fundamental trait of Roman character was reverence for authority, and a habit of absolute obedience. This was the developing principle in the formation of the national life. To the Roman boy, the father of the family was the expression of absolute authority (the Roman father had the power of life and death over his children); when the boy became a man, the state bore to him a similar relation. He in Rome was most virtuous, most excellent, who advanced in the highest degree the welfare of the state; and since conquest was the prevailing aim of the state, personal bravery and military prowess became the chief good. This for a time produced a sturdy type of character, the valiant Roman. But as soon as the state itself became corrupt, as soon as the fathers themselves became weaklings, reverence for law and authority died, and Rome

rotted. External law proved insufficient to change the life, to restrain from sin, or to renew the heart.

3. The Jews: Again, the Jewish people were given by God a special capacity for religion, and were taken by him to be the chosen medium of revelation by means of the preparatory system of Judaism. Judaism was a religion largely of externals; of rites and ceremonies; pictures, to be sure, of high spiritual realities, but not given as a final religion, or as an ultimate solution of the question of moral motive power. It was only preparatory. In the far-reaching providence of God, it was used to demonstrate the insufficiency of the blood of bulls and goats, as an offering for sin, and of external rites and ceremonies, as a motive power to uplift to holiness, no matter how grand, imposing and awe-inspiring these rites and ceremonies might be. The law was, as Paul has told us, only a school-master to lead us unto Christ. It was never intended as a sufficient motive power to change the life, to restrain from sin, or to renew the heart.

Thus was the world prepared by three great failures to witness the fact of one magnificent success.

ONE GREAT SUCCESS

In the fullness of time Christ came to an expectant but sin-beclouded world. To a world that had witnessed the failure of culture, the height of attainment of law, and the impotence of ritual; to a weary, disappointed, sin-enslaved world, needing, oh! so sadly, some mighty motive power which should come down with the omnipotence of God, and lift up fallen and falling humanity to a higher, purer air. To such a world, God came in the person of Jesus Christ. God, not now "The Unknowable," far removed beyond the ken of man; not a God of Mystery enshrined in a secret Holy of Holies, and approached only through symbolic sacrifices and clouds of incense; but God manifest in the flesh—God with us, Immanuel, in human form, with human sympathies, and in intimate relationship with men. And as Jesus, Son of God and Son of Man, "went about doing good," he said to those who had failed to find elsewhere a sufficient force to uplift, "Follow me"; and to those wearied by futile efforts to find release from self and sin, "Come unto me, all ye who labor and are heavy laden, and I will give you rest. Take my yoke upon you and learn of me, for I am meek and lowly in heart, and ye shall find rest unto your souls." To the darkness of the world he said, "I am the light of the world." To those seeking truth he said, "I am the way, the truth and the life"; and speaking of the power which his life and death were to have in the world, he said, "And I, if I be lifted up, will draw all men unto me." Three and a half years were thus spent in intimate contact with men, during which he continually referred to himself as the one source of light and life. And when, at the end of his earthly ministry in the flesh, he hung upon the cross; when Greece with culture, and Rome with external law, and the Hebrews with ritual had failed to save; in the day of his apparent defeat, but of his real victory, these three great nations of antiquity bore unwilling witness to their own insufficiency and to his almightiness, when, over that cross on Golgotha, it was written in Greek, in Latin, and in Hebrew, "This is Jesus, the King of the Jews." Here is a motive sufficient. Here is power. Here is the King. Three days he lay in the grave, after which he arose from the dead, because the tomb could no longer hold him. During the space of forty days he showed himself alive to his brethren, and talked with them concerning the things of the Kingdom; and when at last he left for a time their mortal vision, he said, "Go, carry on my work in my strength, for lo, I (in the person of the Holy Spirit) am with you all the days." So they went forth to their work, walking and talking with Jesus, living and working daily in constant and conscious communion with the Spirit, and under the impetus of his love for them and their love for him. So also Paul, having been converted at the sight of this same Jesus, was consumed with love for him; was driven on from place to place in zealous activity and service; impelled by a personal, passionate attachment for Christ. In his second letter to the Corinthians he explains the secret of his zeal by the words of the text, "For the love of Christ constraineth us; because we thus judge, that one died for all, therefore all died; and he died for all, that they who live should no longer live unto themselves, but unto him who for their sake died and rose again." Here, then, is the motive power, "The love of Christ."

Thus we see that the power of Christianity was not to be the power of a creed, nor the power of a ritual, nor even (I say it reverently) the power of a book; but the power of a person. Christ in us. The source, center and goal of Christianity is Christ. Christ is Christianity. Strange is it that a part of the church should have for so long a time lost sight of this fact, and buried the Christ under ritual and creed and ceremony. A hopeful sign is it for church and college and the world, when from all sides in these thoughtful days, when men are trying to find the secret of our lack of power; a hopeful sign is it, when high theologians and humble evangelists, devout students and a hungry church, all unite in the agonizing cry, "Back to Christ, give us Christ, we must re-discover Christ." To those who inquire, "Why is not the church more powerful? why are so many Christians without power?" the sorrowful answer of Mary is heard in reply, "Because they have taken away my Lord and I know not where they have laid him." The person of Christ is the motive power in Christianity. Personality is always power and the only real power. The history of the world reveals the power of personality. The history of the world is but the history of a few great men. History is mostly biography. Men make history. The history of missions reveals the power of personality. The history of education bears witness to the same fact, the power of persons. The history of revelation reveals the same fact. The Bible is not an abstract statement of theology. A large part of the Bible is history; much of it simply biography. God has revealed truth through men. Men live truth, thus truth becomes alive and powerful, because personal. So in Christianity, the center and source of power is the Person of Jesus Christ.

THE POWER OF CHRIST

1. Now, the power of Christ depends first upon his character and work. The amount of power which any one has in this world, other things being equal, is in proportion to the purity and sincerity of one's life. Dear friends, young and old, let us never forget this. You and I will have power in this world, other things being equal, to

the degree that our lives are pure and sincere. In proportion as these elements of purity and sincerity are lacking, power will be lacking. Let us recall the purity and sincerity of the life of Christ. He could always meet the opposition of his foes with the brave challenge, "Who convicteth me of sin?" It is sincerity that gives courage and power. The insincere man is always a coward. "Conscience doth make cowards of us all." Christ could teach the highest precepts with absolute authority, because his practice always accorded with his precepts. He was the most influential teacher that ever lived, not simply on account of the substance of his teaching, but because he was the only teacher who ever lived whose life was equal to his highest precepts. There is something irresistibly attractive in real goodness, and Christ by the power of his purity and the sincerity of his life has ever been winning new friends to himself.

And then not only the purity and sincerity of his life gave him power, but also the character of his work gave him great power. His whole life was unselfish, his whole work was for others, a life of unselfish devotion to the good of men. He it was who made it clear that he is greatest who serves most his fellows, he is most powerful who suffers most for others' good. Gratitude has always been a most powerful basis of appeal, and Christ gained power over men by doing things for men. The most significant comment upon his life ever written was, "He went about doing good." He put men under obligation to himself by the favors which he did them; while his crowning work of sacrifice of self upon the cross for men's sins, must ever be a source of tremendous power. Christ's resurrection also from the dead and the power of an eternal life have given him a great hold upon men. We do not worship a dead Christ, but a living Christ. Buddha in leaving his followers at his death did indeed with sadness say, "Your teacher you will no longer have, but I will leave you my teachings." But Christ, when about to depart for a time from mortal vision, triumphantly said, "Lo, I am with you alway." He ever liveth to make intercession for us, and through us he still pleads with men.

2. But the power of the person of Christ depends not simply upon his character and work, but also upon the intimacy and character of the relationship established between himself and men. This relationship was of the most intimate kind. In Christ we have not Plato's God, afar off and unknowable; not a God "sitting on the outer rim of the Universe and watching it spin," but God in intimate relationship and sympathy with men. He took upon himself all of man's limitations; he was tempted and tried in all points like as we are; he entered into every

human experience, tasted the joys and sorrows common to the race. He literally put himself into man's place, and lived as a man among men. And then he said to his followers, "I call you not servants, but I have called you friends; for all things that I have heard of my Father I have made known unto you." "My Father and I desire to live on very close terms with you; we desire to come in and sup with you and abide with you, and we desire you to abide with us. The bond of love is to be the tie between us." Ah! here was a motive power indeed! Cold, critical culture never saves anybody. Never has, never will, never can. We are apt sometimes to think, or to wish, that the world might be ruled by reason, or logic; but 'tis not so, 'twill never be so. Life is greater than learning; heart is mightier than head; love is stronger than logic. And the poet has done well to sing:

> "Ah, how skillful grows the hand
> That obeyeth love's command!
> 'Tis the heart and not the brain
> That to the highest doth attain;
> And he who followeth Love's behest
> Far excelleth all the rest."

Here, then, in our text Paul has given us the secret of power in Christianity, "The love of Christ constrains us." Christ's love for us, as shown in his self-denying life and sacrificial death; and our love for him, aroused by his own moral worthiness, the benefits conferred and the kindnesses done, must ever be the motive power, the driving force, which impels us by love's own sweet compulsion to more and more zeal in his service, and to efforts for those for whom he died. Here, then, in such a personality, and in such a bond of relationship, is a mighty motive power, the best that God in his wisdom and mercy could provide; but somehow we don't seem to have in our churches the power which we should have. You have not in your church the power you ought to have. Why is it? In what does the power of a church consist? The power of a church is the sum total of the personal powers of each of the members, plus that increment of power which comes from union. Just this; no more, no less. You, then, individually are responsible for a part of the lack of power. You, then, individually are able to add to the power by increasing the power of your own Christian life. This may be done in two ways. First, we must come into more intimate relationship with Christ, the source of power. We need to get full of God's spirit, and then we'll have influence, then we'll have power. We need to be on fire for God. We must remove from our lives those things which hinder our growth in grace, which interfere with our freedom in prayer and in service; those selfish indulgences, those un-Christlike things, which mar our spiritual lives and lessen our power with God and man. Then, by reading God's book and thinking God's thoughts, by prayer and meditation, and by activity in his service, we need to be drawn more closely to him.

But not only the relationship Godward needs renewing and strengthening; we must also come into more intimate contact with men, if we are to have power over them. We hear much about the separation of the church from the masses. If they are separated from each other, they never became separated *en masse*. They become separated as individuals. They must be brought together as individuals. Pharisaism by its separation could never save the world, but Christianity by personal contact of Christlike individuals with individuals, can and must save the race. Men are not saved at a distance, but by personal contact with saved men, who reveal to them a living, present and powerful Savior. If we would have power, then, we must come into most intimate relationship with Christ, the source of power, and with those whom we would save.

Some years ago I looked upon an interesting picture. In the foreground was the ocean, stirred by a storm, its billows tossing mountain high; while in the background was a rocky shore, and upon its crags a large cross, to which was clinging the form of a woman, just rescued from a watery grave. Ah! it was a beautiful sight; for, with both arms firmly clasped about the cross, she looked heavenward with beaming face and read on the sky the song of her soul, "Simply to thy cross I cling." This, I thought, was a Christian masterpiece; until some time afterwards I saw another picture which excelled the first as sunlight exceeds the light of the stars. In the foreground there was the same storm-swept ocean, in the background the craggy shore, the cross and the inspiring motto; while a woman just rescued from the deep, clung with one arm only to the cross, and, with face heavenward and seaward, stretched out the other arm to those who were perishing in the same sea from which she had scarcely been saved. Ah! methinks the latter is Christianity! Not both arms about a cross, and ecstasy over personal salvation, forgetful of the peril of others; but with a firm grasp upon the cross with one arm, with face Christward and manward, the other stretched out to save our fellows. With one hand in the hand of the sinless, and the other hand in the hand of the sinner, let us in Christ's stead beseech men to be reconciled to God. So shall the Person of Christ be the motive power in our lives, and become the loving Savior of others.

Gradual Growth

Mark 4: 28.—"First the blade, then the ear, after that the full corn in the ear."

OUR Lord spoke three parables about the Kingdom of God with reference to the subject of growth.*

(a) At one time he said, "The Kingdom of God is like a grain of mustard seed, which, when it is sown in the earth, is less than all the seeds that be in the earth; but when it is sown, it groweth up and becometh greater than all herbs and shooteth out great branches, so that the fowls of the air may lodge under the shadow of it." By this parable Christ represented the Kingdom of God as an external society, beginning small and increasing in size, and growth in the Kingdom as something external and visible, resulting in increased bulk.

(b) Again, our Savior likened the Kingdom of God to "leaven, which a woman took, and hid in

---

* Again I desire to express my great debt to the writings of Prof. A. B. Bruce.

three measures of meal, till the whole was leavened." In this parable the Kingdom of God is represented as an internal force; and growth in it as something internal, invisible, resulting in a transformed mass.

(c) Again, our Savior said, "So is the Kingdom of God, as if a man should cast seed into the ground; and should sleep and rise, night and day, and the seed should spring and grow up, he knoweth not how. For the earth bringeth forth fruit of herself; first the blade, then the ear, after that the full corn in the ear. But when the fruit is ripe, immediately he putteth in the sickle, because the harvest is come." In this parable emphasis is laid upon the nature of growth, as something mysterious, something spontaneous, and something gradually progressive.

It is necessary in the interpretation of all illustrations, comparisons and parables, carefully to recognize the difference between that which is essential and that which is incidental, between figure and shading, foreground and background. For instance, when our Lord's second coming is likened unto the coming of a thief in the night, it is evident that the thing taught is not that he shall necessarily come at night time, nor that he shall use the devices of a thief, but that he shall come suddenly and unexpectedly. Now, in the parable above mentioned, of "the blade, the ear, and the full corn in the ear," it is evident that "the casting of the seed into the ground," and "the putting in of the sickle when harvest time has come," are but shading to round out and complete the picture. Three things seem to stand in the foreground and to be emphasized: The mysteriousness of growth, "it springeth and groweth up and he knoweth not how"; the spontaneity of growth, "the earth bringeth forth fruit of herself"; and the gradual progressiveness of growth, "first the blade, then the ear, after that the full corn in the ear." As to which of these three ideas was predominating in the mind of the Savior at the time of utterance, if indeed any one was foremost in his mind, may be a matter for difference of opinion or interpretation; but to my own mind the thought of the gradual progressiveness of growth is the more prominent, and the phrases, "first the blade, then the ear, after that the full corn in the ear," are the more emphatic. Allow me, then, to take the clauses, "first the blade, then the ear, after that the full corn in the ear," as a text, and to call your attention to the law of gradual and progressive growth.

1. We note first that this law is easily recognized as a law always operative in the natural, physical world. In the springtime, as processes move on before our very eyes, we see the erstwhile leafless and apparently lifeless trees, under the influence of warmth, sunshine and rain, begin to bud and to blush with the might of life.

As night and day, sunshine and shade follow, the buds develop and burst into fragrant bloom, green fruit and shade-giving leaf. Summer follows spring, and the gradually progressive process goes on, until the ripening days of autumn bring processes to fruition and the development is complete. Among animals, also, there is the spring of childhood, the summer of youth and middle age, and the autumn of maturity. In the vegetable and animal worlds alike, i. e., wherever there is life and growth, the law of the gradualness and progressiveness of growth is seen.

But Christian apologists, while easily admitting the existence of such laws in the natural world, have been slow to admit their existence in the world of spiritual things. There has been manifested a certain fearfulness, lest if there should be admitted the existence in spiritual things of laws, of such things as cause and effect, the spiritual might be debased to the level of the natural. There has been a fear, lest if natural laws were admitted to have counterparts, or analogous laws, in the spiritual realm, the spiritual might become natural, law and order might be enthroned as God, and the Creator ruled entirely out of the Universe. And yet, what seems more reasonable than that he, who established the laws of nature, should have established similar laws in the world of spirit. Must the supernatural be necessarily contrary to nature, and miracle be equivalent to magic? However, such reasonings are rapidly passing away, and a wider scholarship and a more tolerant age have given us a new point of view. To-day we everywhere recognize in spiritual things the existence of laws, laws which in many cases seem to be analogous to, or identical with, the laws of the natural world. Let us consider the oneness of this law of gradualness and progressiveness of growth in Creation, Revelation and Sanctification.

2. Creation was gradual and progressive. I am not advocating that theory of so-called evolution which would make the ape the remote ancestor of man. For over against a century of theorizing and experimentation to support such a theory of evolution, must be written the verdict, "Not proven." No well differentiated species has ever been produced. Interesting varieties have been developed; but a fatal law of atavism has always brought about a reversion to the original type. Connecting links have either been lost, or never existed. In the mineral world, however, we have preserved to us the record in geological strata of the gradual preparation of the earth for man. But whatever may be one's theory of evolution, whether it were a true evolution or by distinct creative acts; creation was, at any rate, probably a gradual and progressive process. This is not only not contrary to, but in exact accord

with, the general teaching of the program of creation, presented to us in the first chapter of Genesis. First God existed. Then the heavens and the earth were created, without form and void, enveloped in darkness, but under the brooding spirit of the Almighty. Then light, a first necessity of life, was created. Then heaven, earth, dry land, sea, night and day were separated. Then vegetable life appeared. Then the lower animal life and fishes. Then quadrupeds and the higher vertebrates, and finally man. Thus the process was a gradually progressive one, leading from lower to higher, culminating in man, the highest of all. The law of creation was "First the blade, then the ear, after that the full corn in the ear."

3. Again, Revelation was gradual and progressive. God did not reveal the whole of his will to any one of the prophets or apostles, nor at any one time. His revelation proceeded upon true principles of education, beginning with the simple and proceeding to the profound; from concrete to abstract; from pictured truth to spiritual reality. That this was the method of revelation may be illustrated in many ways. Take, for example, the emphasis placed at first upon outward forms and ceremonies. Note how much was made at first of ritual; how only gradually the prophets rose to higher spiritual perceptions, and the truth was emphasized, "To

obey is better than sacrifice, and to hearken than the fat of rams." Gradually the internal rose above the external, the spiritual above the material. Christ referred to this gradually progressive process in revelation when he said to the woman of Samaria, "The hour cometh when ye shall neither in this mountain, nor yet at Jerusalem, worship the Father. But the hour cometh, and now is, when the true worshipers shall worship the Father in spirit and in truth; for the Father seeketh such to worship him. God is a spirit; and they that worship must worship in spirit and in truth." Again, note how at first in Scripture the rewards for piety are largely material things; while, in the full light of completed revelation, the highest rewards of piety and the fruits of the spirit are spiritual blessings. Again, note the gradualness and progressiveness in the revelation of certain great ideas, such as, for example, the immortality of the soul, and the life beyond the grave. Indeed, there seems to be very little concerning these great subjects in the Old Testament. A glimpse or two in Job, or a hope expressed in a Psalm, is about all. It is only in New Testament times that Christ brought "life and immortality to light, through the Gospel." In nothing is the gradualness and progressiveness of revelation more clearly seen than in the development of Messianic Prophecy, the gradual unfolding of the plan of salvation through a coming Savior. The theme of Redemption begins in Genesis in very indistinct and uncertain tones; and, like the approach of music from afar, only a note here and there in the divine melody can be distinguished. On and on roll the centuries; prophet after prophet arises, each adding some new variation, or modulation, to the original theme. Sometimes, from some mountain peak of prophetic activity, like that of Isaiah, the strains roll majestic, and every note in the divine melody rings out with the clearness of a bell. Sometimes, in some valley of national decay, or prophetic silence, the strains seem to die away, and the music seems muffled. On and on roll the ages, until at last the bugle call announces the birth of John the Baptist, the herald of coming deliverance; and then, on the well known December night, in the fullness of God's time, over the hills of Bethlehem rings out the oratorio of the Messiah, the full Hallelujah Chorus of Redemption, "Glory to God in the highest, and on earth peace, good will to men." Thus from the beginning of the Old Testament Revelation to the coming of Christ, the method of revelation was that of gradual and progressive growth. In the New Testament, likewise, we find the gradually progressive process continued: Christ himself revealing God's will to man "as they were able to bear it"; and the apostles, after the death and resurrection of Christ, explaining, as it was revealed to them, the full meaning of the salvation which the Son had accomplished.

Since Apostolic days, there has been no development in the line of addition of new truths, God's written revelation being complete, a sufficient declaration of his will, and an infallible guide in all matters of faith and practice. In it, and in the divine human character revealed in it, are hidden all the treasures of wisdom and knowledge. In the perception and application of truth, however, the gradually progressive process continues. Every day reveals to us new applications of truth, and new depths and heights and lengths and breadths of his wonderful love and gracious purposes towards mankind. Thus we see that the law of revelation was the law of gradual and progressive growth. "First the blade, then the ear, after that the full corn in the ear."

4. Again, Sanctification is gradual and progressive. In the Kingdom of God, as an external society and as represented by the Church of Christ upon earth, the growth has been a very gradual one; and, as we firmly believe, in general a progressive growth. When one takes a broad and unprejudiced view of the history of the church, of the civilization of which Christianity has been the chief cause; when one sees how one age has led up to and prepared the way for a subsequent and better age; in spite of the dark times, and many

GRADUAL GROWTH

black pages of history, it is easy to sing with the poet:

> "Yet I doubt not through the ages
> One increasing purpose runs,
> And the thoughts of men are widened
> With the process of the suns."

The gradual growth of the power of religious ideas, the increasing hold of the Christ upon men, the slow but sure progress in the regeneration of society, are fascinating themes, and illustrate clearly the law of gradual and progressive growth, but I cannot speak of them now. It is a more personal matter that I wish to consider, and to apply the text to the process of the sanctification of the individual. Nor is it my purpose to discuss the question of the possibility of immediate sanctification, nor the question of the degree of sanctification attainable in this life. Suffice it to say, that, if immediate sanctification in this life has ever taken place, it is not the usual thing, nor the ordinary process of sanctification. I care not to treat of exceptions, but of the general rule. As to the degree of sanctification attainable in this life, it is not a question of degree, but a question of method, with which I am now concerned.

All real growth, all permanent growth is slow growth. The clinging vine may, in a single summer, climb to a great height, but it takes a century to grow an oak. Jonah's gourd came up in a night, but it likewise perished in a night.

The cathedrals of Europe, centuries old, were centuries in building. Again, the higher forms of life are more slow of development. A horse often is at its best in a few years, but a man only attains maturity after several decades. The monad passes through birth, youth, maturity, old age and death, within the short period of twenty-four hours; but it is only a monad. If, then, real growth, permanent growth, is slow, and still more so in proportion as the product is high, must not the development of character, the attainment of sanctification, the winning of that which is highest and best, and toward the attainment of which all noblest endeavors should always be engaged, must not that growth be indeed a slow and a gradual one? Our text suggests three stages of growth in sanctification, a blade stage, a green ear stage, and a full corn stage. (And here Professor Bruce, in his treatment of Christ's parables, is very helpful.) At once several questions arise. Do these three stages always appear in the process of sanctification? Do they always occur in the same order, and are they always distinguishable one from another? As to the last question, it must be noted, referring again to the grain which is the basis of comparison, that growth in the natural world is such a gradually progressive process, that it is not possible to be so minute as to affirm that for just so many days, hours and minutes, grain is in the blade stage; and then, for just so many days, hours and minutes, it is in the green ear stage; and then, for just so many days, hours and minutes, it is in the full corn stage. These stages merge one into another. But, looked at from a more general standpoint, we see that there is a blade period, there is a green ear period, and there is a full corn period. So with these stages in the development of sanctification, one stage merges into another, but in general the three stages occur, and occur in the order named. Let us note some of the characteristics of these stages. Mark the blade period; or, referring to fruit as well as to grain, we may call it the blossom period, the spring-tide, the time of initial growth. It is a time of enthusiasm, of childhood's happy joy, of the wild thrill of first love. And, referring to the beginning period of the Christian's life, we recall the joyousness of the young convert, and the ardent enthusiasm; the zeal which would quickly convert a world, and which stands amazed at the apparent coldness of older Christians; the light step and the bounding joy of a new life. But note also, concerning the very beginning of this initial period, how nature illustrates diverse operations of grace. Some kinds of grain, when planted, make the first show of life by sending up through the clods a little spike of green. There is no demonstration; without observation, almost, the little blade makes its way up to the light and air, and the process of initial growth is a very quiet and unobserved one. But fruit trees, which seemed just a while ago so dead and cold, in a very few days of sunshine swell quickly and, apparently almost in an instant, burst into a halo of bloom, and into a bower of fragrance. So the beginning of the new life is manifested differently in different persons. Some, especially children, accustomed from earliest days to the teachings of the Bible and to thoughts of Christ, are born so quietly into the spiritual world as to realize scarcely any change in condition. Though they have been truly born again, the manifestation of the new life has been so gradual, that, in after days, though they are sure of their having been born again, they are never able to determine the exact time when the new birth took place. Then there are others, and particularly is this true of older people, who, dead in indifference and hardened by years of sin and selfish indulgence, are suddenly arrested in their course of godlessness, catch a saving sight of Jesus, and immediately all is changed. They were lost, but are found. They were dead in sin, but now have begun to live unto Christ. The whole world seems new; the sun shines brighter; the sky is bluer; the grass is greener. Things are the same as of old, but the man has changed. The tree has burst into bloom. But it must always be kept in mind that this blade stage, this blossom period, is but the beginning of the Christian life. Many mistake the blossom for the fruit, springtime for harvest, holy feeling for holy living, gushing enthusiasm for staunch character.

Sooner or later, blade and blossom are followed by green ear and unripe fruit. This is a second stage in the process of sanctification. It is a time of transition. "A time of waiting, of unfulfilled desires, of unrealized ideals, of green ears and unripe fruit, of experiences more profitable than pleasant." The green fruit is a stage in advance of the blossom, but it is not so beautiful or fragrant. The second stage is "a time of temptation and struggle, of doubts and fears, of sadness and gloom." A time when the foundations of faith are re-examined, when deeper views of the meaning of consecration bring doubts as to one's own sincerity, and a higher perception of the demands of holiness brings despair as to one's own attainment. It is a trying time, indeed, a time when many sincere souls sometimes doubt even their own conversion. And yet it is but a preparatory stage to something richer and riper. Let not those who are passing through such experiences be unduly cast down, or too severely blame themselves. It is no sin to be in the "green corn and unripe fruit" stage, though it is sin permanently to remain so, and never to pass beyond from greenness to ripeness. This transition period usually comes to all those who bring forth the best fruit; for always has it been true that "they who reap in greatest joy sow most in tears."

But, as blossom was followed by unripe fruit, and blade by green ear; so surely, if we are faithful and patient, unripe fruit will be followed by ripeness, and green ear by the full corn in the ear. This third stage of sanctification is referred to by Bunyan, when, in the "Pilgrim's Progress," Christian, having passed through the Valley of Humiliation and the Shadow of Death, having escaped the clutches of Giant Despair, has at last reached Beulah Land, from which one cannot so much as see Doubting Castle, and where one lives within constant vision of the Eternal City. Here the fruit of the spirit has become an abiding possession. "Love, joy, peace, long-suffering," have become traits of character, and "heavenly impulse has become a heavenly habit." Those who attain to this stage of Christian maturity are always conscious of the high demands of holiness, of their constant dependence upon Christ, of the heinousness of sin, and are clearly cognizant of their own shortcomings.

Thus the course of personal sanctification is seen to be a gradual and progressive one. "First the blade, then the ear, after that the full corn in the ear."

As the process of sanctification is slow and

GRADUAL GROWTH

gradual, as there are stages which must necessarily be passed through, we need to exercise continually the Christlike virtue of patience. First, patience with others. How crude and immature the ideas of some seem to be! How full of glaring faults their lives are! Why cannot they see that such actions are so un-Christlike! But we must exercise patience! How patient the Master was with those rude fishermen, his disciples, whose ideas seemed so worldly, whose ambitions were so sordid, whose passions were so uncontrolled, who were so slow to believe and to understand the parables and spiritual truths which he wished to teach them! And yet the Master never lost his patience. And then we must be patient with ourselves. We become impatient of slow processes. We crave short-cuts to holiness and fruitfulness. But we shall attain to highest maturity only as we patiently abide God's time and faithfully perform the duties of each day. Those who were profitable hearers received the word into good and honest hearts, and "with patience brought forth fruit unto perfection." "Let us also, then, laying aside every weight and the sin that doth so easily beset us, run with patience the race that is set before us, looking unto Jesus, the author and finisher of our faith." Thus may we all, "beholding as in a mirror the glory of the Lord, be changed into the same image from glory to glory," and then, when the gradually progressive process of sanctification is complete, and we pass into his presence, "we shall be satisfied when we awake in his likeness."

Working for Jesus

Matt. 25:15.—"And unto one he gave five talents, to another two, to another one; to each according to his several ability; and he went on his journey."

OUR Savior spoke three parables upon the great theme of "Work and Wages in the Kingdom of God": the parable of the husbandman, hiring laborers to work in his vineyard; the parable of the ten pounds, given to the ten servants; and the parable of the talents. The parable of the talents is doubtless, to many of us, the most familiar of the three. Its lessons have often been considered, and yet it may be of great profit to us to recall at this time some of its most evident teachings.

The parable story is briefly told. A man of some wealth is about to go to a distant country. He leaves his money and property in the hands of his servants *for use*. The ability of each of his servants is well known to him. Being a wise manager, he does not give similar amounts to all, but gives to each according to each one's ability;

not too much to any, not too little to any; to none enough to burden or overcome, to none so little as to encourage to idleness; but "unto one he gave five talents, to another two, to another one; to each according to his several ability; and he went on his journey." As soon as the master was gone, the first servant, by prudent business methods, by looking for and seizing every possible opportunity, by constant diligence and skill, succeeded in doubling his capital. The second servant, who had received two talents, manifested a similar diligence and skill, and achieved a similar result, the doubling of his capital. The third servant was a timid and shrinking man, of less ability than either of the others, but *able to do something;* with a poor opinion of his master and of himself, lazy as well as little and lean. This one went away and dug a hole in the ground and "hid his lord's money." "After a long time, the lord of those servants cometh and reckoneth with them." After a long time! After sufficient time has passed for testing the diligence and efficiency of each servant; after sufficient time for each one to have had splendid opportunities for accomplishing something for the master, the lord of those servants returns, and each one is called to give an account of his stewardship. The man who had received the five talents comes forward, with beaming face and firm step, proud of his honest achievement, and yet humble with the humility so becoming a faithful servant; and says, "Lord, thou deliveredst unto me five talents; behold, I have gained beside them five talents more." The master rejoices in such a servant, and his bounding heart responds to such service, "Well done" (had he not done well?) "thou good and faithful servant; thou hast been faithful over a few things; I will make thee ruler over many things: enter thou into the joy of thy lord." After this servant comes another, the one who had received two talents. He, also, has a happy face, and a throbbing heart, as the result of faithful living, already possessing a heaven of happiness as the result of conscious attainment and humble gratitude for the privilege of service. "He also that had received two talents came and said, 'Lord, thou deliveredst unto me two talents: behold, I have gained two other talents beside them.'" Again appears the master's responsive smile, and again are heard the words of approval, "Well done, good and faithful servant; thou hast been faithful over a few things; I will make thee ruler over many things: enter thou into the joy of thy lord." Thus far, the day of reckoning has been a day of honest joy, both to master and servants; a day when the seal of divine approval has but brought added delight to those who have already known the privilege and pleasure of faithful living. But *now* comes one whose unfaithfulness has brought shadow and shame upon himself, and who carries gloom wherever he goes. "Then he that had received the one talent came and said, 'Lord, I knew thee, that thou art an hard man, reaping where thou hast not sown, and gathering where thou hast not scattered: and I was afraid, and went and hid thy talent in the earth: lo, there thou hast that is thine.' His lord answered and said unto him, 'Thou wicked and slothful servant, thou knewest that I reap where I sowed not, and gather where I have not scattered: thou oughtest therefore to have put my money to the exchangers, and then at my coming I should have received my own with interest. Thou oughtest to have been afraid to have appeared before me empty handed.'" If too timid to take responsibility and too lazy to work, you could at least have put my money to the exchangers for interest. There is *no excuse for your having done absolutely nothing.* "Cast ye the unprofitable servant into outer darkness: there shall be weeping and gnashing of teeth." Cast him out! Let the gloom which he has made for himself be perpetual. Cast him out! There shall be weeping and gnashing of teeth, weeping over lost opportunities, and gnashing of teeth in envy of those who, by faithfulness, won what he might have had. This is the parable story briefly told and paraphrased; let us now note some of the more apparent teachings:

1. *The master expects service from every one of*

his servants. (a) The very idea of a kingdom suggests a king and subjects, implying loyalty and allegiance. (b) A talent was given to every one; every one was called to an account, because the master expected something from every one of his servants. (c) Paul loved to call himself the "bond servant" of Jesus Christ, declaring that he was not his own, but had been bought with a price. We have all of us as Christians been set free from the slavery of sin, that we may be servants of righteousness and of him who redeemed us, not "with corruptible things, as silver and gold, . . . but with the precious blood of Christ, as of a lamb without blemish and without spot." (d) One purpose of the Lord's delayed coming is that every one may have a splendid opportunity for service; no one will be able to say at that time, "O Lord, you came back too soon. I didn't get a chance or time to render any service." (e) The very purpose of our endowments and relationships is that we may use all of these things for God. We are stewards in respect to all things that we possess, and it is required of stewards that a man be found faithful. (f) It is God's design to use men and women in the accomplishment of his purposes. No angel will be sent down to do in your community what God expects you and calls you to do. (g) The Master expects service not simply from ministers and trained workers, but from every one of his servants. The parable as recorded in Mark says: "To every man his work." If you are a son, then the message of the Master to you is, "Son, go work to-day in my vineyard." "And let him that heareth say 'Come'." (h) There is no place for idlers in the Kingdom of God. The Master seems continually to be going about and saying, "Why stand ye here the whole day idle? There's work to be done. There's a harvest to be gathered. Loafers are not wanted!" Drones were, in ancient times, "drummed out of camp." (i) If Christ is in you, he will manifest himself, and will cry out as of old, "I must be about my Father's business." If you are doing nothing for Christ you may well doubt whether the Christ is in you. If there is not in you some divine compulsion, driving you on in the Master's service, you may be sure that there is not much of the Christ in you. You may well doubt whether you are a Christian. And, what is more, if you are doing nothing *for* him, you *will* soon doubt whether you are in him: for idleness is the sure road to doubt and despair. (j) There is no excuse for doing absolutely nothing. The servant of least ability, with only one talent, had at least the exchangers. Whatever these exchangers may represent in the opportunities of to-day, the teaching is very clear that even he had no excuse for having done absolutely nothing. No one of God's children is doomed to idleness in his vineyard. (k) The servant who went away and dug a hole in the ground and "hid his lord's money," withdrew so much money from active circulation, and embarrassed to that extent the affairs of Christ's kingdom. During a recent campaign in our political world, people were denouncing most severely all measures which would tend to a contraction of the currency, and were heaping blessings upon the heads of any whose policy would honestly and surely increase the volume of the circulating medium. All people, irrespective of party affiliations, were agreed that the contraction of the currency and hard times had a close connection with one another, whatever may have been the cause of the contraction. Money had been very seriously withdrawn from the avenues of trade. Hard times had come with the stringency in the money-market. Something must be done to bring back into circulation a larger amount of the medium of exchange. When money should begin again to circulate freely, good times would return. The Kingdom of God is suffering in many places from a contraction of the circulating medium. I speak not particularly with reference to money in the Kingdom. I refer to your hands, your feet, your voices, yourselves. They are the circulating medium by which our King does business. There is "hard times" in the Kingdom to-day, because you have withdrawn these things from the King's service. You, your voices, your feet, your hands, your influence, your time, these are God's medium of exchange, by which he designs to carry on his business. Do you wish to know how to bring about a revival in the religious life of your community? There is but one sure way. Let there be a return of confidence, on the part of Christians, in God's Book, in God's power and willingness to save through Christ, in God's promises, in his purpose to use you, each one of you, in some part of this work, in the superlative worth of the soul of every man, and in his capacity for redemption. Let there be on your part a return of confidence in these things, and then invest—invest your every power! Consecrate every relationship to God. Put into circulation in God's Kingdom your all; and there'll be a mighty revival, not only in your own personal life, but also in your community.

2. The Master *expects a peculiar service from every one* of his servants. "Unto one he gave five talents, to another two, to another one; to each according to his several ability"; or, as Mark says, "To each man his work." (a) All of the Master's servants are expected to serve him, but they are not all expected to serve him in a similar capacity, or in the same way. To each person special duties and special privileges come. No two persons are exactly alike in ability or circumstances. We are not blocks of uniform size, not things, but persons. God has so honored the

individual as to have made each one of us differ in some respect from every other one. God never made two *persons* exactly alike. Individuality is stamped upon every member of the human race. We are born as individuals. We die as individuals. We are saved as individuals. Christ loves us as individuals. We shall be judged as individuals. "For we must all appear before the judgment-seat of Christ, that every one may receive the things done in his body, according to that which he hath done, whether it be good or bad." Thus we have peculiar privileges and peculiar perils, and from each one the Master expects peculiar service. (b) In the recognition of this fact lies the true division of labor in both the religious and economic worlds. One of the most common causes of unrest and disaster in the economic world, is the failure to realize that the true division of labor is grounded in capacity and circumstance. There are so many "misfits" in life; men in the law who ought to be in the ministry; men in the ministry who ought to be in the law; men in the country who ought to be in the town, and in the town who ought to be in the country; men in business who ought to be in the professions, and men in the professions who ought to be in commercial life, etc., etc. Solomon's proverb, so often mistranslated and misapplied, "Train up a child according to his way" (to his bent), "and when he is old he will not depart from it," furnishes a true principle of education; and, in the future, we may hope that our youth shall be clearly taught the real basis of all true division of labor, as grounded in capacity and circumstance. Then, in the future, so many "misfits" will not occur. When the millennium shall have come in the economic world, every man and woman will be doing that which he is best fitted to do. So, in the religious world, the true division of labor lies in capacity and circumstance. Not all are called to preach from the pulpit; not all are to call upon the sick; not all are to teach in the Sunday-school. The church, according to Paul's inimitable figure, is one body, many members. "For the body is not one member, but many. And if they were all one member, where were the body? But now hath God set the members each one of them in the body, even as it pleased him, and the eye cannot say to the hand, I have no need of thee: or again, the head to the feet, I have no need of thee. Nay, much rather, those members of the body which seem to be more feeble are necessary. Now ye are the body of Christ, and members each in his part." Each one of us has a peculiar work to do, and the work of each is necessary to the completeness of the whole. (c) Through peculiar service from each servant, Christ's far-reaching purposes will best be fulfilled. The Master desires that his Kingdom shall reach persons of every profession and calling, of every class and circumstance: consequently he wishes to have workers in every honorable walk of life. You can work for Christ to better advantage in the sphere of your secular calling than anywhere else, and to better advantage than any one else. The Christian lawyer can have more influence in bringing the unconverted lawyer to Christ than can anybody else. The consecrated physician can have more influence over his non-Christian, professional associates than can any one else. The whole-hearted, devoted Christian clerk can have more influence for Christ over his fellow-clerks than can any one else. So in case of wife or husband, brother or friend. You, if your life is as it ought to be, will have most influence over those who know you best. Knowledge begets confidence. (d) Whatever your future sphere of labor may be, your present one ought to be perfectly plain. *Do the next thing.* Tell the next man what you know about Jesus. O Gadarene! "Go to thy house unto thy friends, and tell them how great things the Lord hath done for thee, and how he had mercy on thee." Begin at home, and in your own community, and among your own friends, to work for Jesus; and when, by patient labor, you have exhausted the possibilities of that sphere, and by faithfulness have manifested your fitness for another, God will surely open up to you new fields of labor. Begin just where you are. Andrew! bring Peter. Philip! bring Nathaniel. Use the opportunities which are now in sight, and your vision will become keener, and you'll soon see more. To the one who uses what he has, will more be given. (e) In faithfully recognizing that Christ's demands are for peculiar service from each one of us lies the secret of much true contentment and joy in life. Let me illustrate this point by referring to an incident which happened some years ago. It was in the summer of 1890, at New Haven, Conn. Rev. R. T. Vann was supplying, during the pastor's absence, the pulpit of the Calvary Baptist Church. Mr. Vann, when twelve years of age, in attempting to help his father in North Carolina, had fallen into a sorghum machine, and had lost both of his arms, one at the shoulder and the other at the elbow. At the time of my meeting him in New Haven, I was well and strong, in the flush of health, and had hardly known what it was to be sick a day in my life. His peace and happiness in his armless state were a continual surprise to me, and I asked him one day, "Don't you often wish, Mr. Vann, that you, like the rest of us, had two arms?" I shall never forget his reply. It impressed me at the time as being absolutely sincere, and in recent years I have learned for myself the secret of his peace. "No, I don't waste time in wishing that any more. I have learned to get along without arms. It would be a great convenience to have one hand with which to write, specially to my dear wife (I can only write a little with the hook on the stub of arm that is left); often there are so many things I should like to tell her, but she has learned to read between the lines. And then, too, when I go to call on my people, it would be a great convenience if I could shake them by the hand; it isn't much pleasure for them to shake an empty coat sleeve. No, I've learned to get along without arms, and to be very happy and contented. Not to have any arms hinders me, too, in my preaching, but then, I've learned some things. You know, Mr. S., God never intended me to be a Spurgeon or a Beecher. He simply wishes *me* to make the most out of the stuff that he has given to *me*. I have long ago learned to thank God that I was nobody but R. T. Vann; if you don't understand what I mean now, before you are as old as I am you will, I trust, have learned its meaning" (his words now seem like prophecy), "and when I get up to the bar of God, I trust that then I can honestly say, 'Lord, here's old, armless R. T. Vann. I have honestly tried, Lord, to make the most out of what you gave me; it's been a pleasure to serve you.' If, at that day, I can say that, will not the Master be pleased?" This was the substance of his answer to my question, and then and there I began to see that, in the clear recognition of the fact that the

Master expects peculiar service from each one of his servants, lies the secret of much real happiness and joy in life.

3. This parable of the talents brings out very clearly also another lesson. Not only does the Master expect service from every one of his servants, and peculiar service from each one of his servants, but also, in this service, *much will depend upon the spirit of the servant, and the spirit of the servant will depend much upon his conception of his master.* One of the most blessed and far-reaching thoughts which ever enter the mind of man is a true thought of God. Man's work and man's character are largely determined by his thought of God. As he gets a true vision of God, man's character is ennobled and his work proves inspiring. As he gets a false view of God, man's character is marred, and the service of God becomes drudgery. One of these servants had a very poor opinion of his master, which opinion made him a very poor servant, and robbed his master of his service. The servant who said, "I knew thee, that thou art an hard man, reaping where thou hast not sown, and gathering where thou hast not scattered," was the servant who went away and dug in the ground, and hid his lord's money. So some people think of God as a hard taskmaster, as a cruel, arbitrary ruler, as a stern judge, before whom we must appear, one who has no personal interest in us except such as

a slave-driver, to get out of us as much as possible. One with such an idea of God, if he ever works for him at all, works as the slave works, from fear, doing only what may be compulsory, and dodging as much work as possible. Such a service is dull, dreary, dry drudgery, with little spirit and no real joy. The biblical conception of God, however, is far different from this. The great God at the center of the universe is not a monster, not a cruel, arbitrary taskmaster, but a gracious Father. He loves every member of the human race. He is personally interested in every one of his creatures. He loves us with an outreaching, overflowing love. He has provided salvation for all in the sacrifice of his Son. "As many as received him, to them gave he the power (authority, right) to become the sons of God." He has redeemed us with his own precious blood, bought us out of the slavery of sin and called us into his own service. He places upon us responsibilities, and gives unto us the privileges of service, for the purpose of developing us. He is not a cruel taskmaster, trying to get out of us as much as possible. He is a loving Father, anxious to make of us as much as possible. It is a great privilege to work for him. Faithful service will bring manifold and abundant reward, both here and hereafter. This was Paul's idea of God, so strikingly set forth in his letter to the Philippians. The thought is this: God is my

Friend, my Father. Christ has redeemed me with his precious blood, has bought me with a great price for his very own, has saved me for a great purpose, is ambitious for me, more so than I am even for myself, has in his heart a large ideal for me. (There is a life-plan in the heart of the Father for each one of his children.) Oh! Father, help me so to live and learn, so to aspire and to act, as that I may not mar or cramp, warp or dwarf the life-plan, the manhood, the character to which thou wouldst have me attain. Help me to realize, to make my own, to seize, "to apprehend that for which also I have been apprehended of Christ Jesus." Father, help me this one thing to do, "forgetting those things which are behind and reaching forth unto those things which are before," to press toward "the mark for the prize of the upward calling of God in Christ Jesus." In joy or sorrow, in pain or pleasure, in prosperity or adversity, "for me to live is Christ, to die is gain." And so "I am in a strait betwixt two things, having a desire to depart and be with Christ (which is far better), nevertheless to abide in the flesh is more needful for you." I stand between two mountain peaks of blessing. Two great boons loom up before me: to live for Christ, to reproduce the Christlike character, to win fruit for eternity; or to die and be forever with Christ. Both are rare privileges indeed, either is a pleasure worth pursuing. How shall I choose? This is the spirit of Paul, the willing servant of Jesus Christ. The slave serves from fear; the hireling serves for money; the son serves from love. "If ye know these things, blessed" (happy) "are ye if ye do them."

The Bible, the Word of God

Isaiah 40:8.—"*The grass withereth, the flower fadeth, but the Word of our God shall stand forever.*"
Matt. 24:35.—"*Heaven and earth shall pass away, but My words shall not pass away.*"

IN this age of books, the truth of Sir Walter Scott's statement, "There is but one book," constantly becomes more apparent. Every year witnesses an increasing amount of devout, searching and systematic study of the Bible. This study assumes various forms—the study of the text, the study of the literary form, the historical study of the source and character of the material, the exegetical study of the meaning, and the devotional study for the upbuilding of the spiritual life. This study of the Bible, specially the historical study, has given rise to many questions which have been popularized through magazines, lecture bureaus, and some pulpits, and which have unnecessarily disturbed the minds and hearts of not a few of God's people. For instance, "What is the date and composition of the Pentateuch, the first five books of the Bible? Did Moses write them, or are they of composite authorship? Or, again, did David write all of the Psalms ascribed to him in the Psalter, or were many of them written by others, and ascribed by tradition to David? Did Isaiah write all of the book which is called by his name, or did one man write the first thirty-nine chapters, and another, living one hundred and fifty years after, write the last twenty-seven chapters? Is the book of Zechariah a unit, or were there two Zechariahs? How many letters were written by the Apostle Paul? Who was the author of Hebrews?" These are a few of the questions that are being discussed in many places, and are disturbing the faith of some. And yet, all of these questions are matters of relatively minor importance; many of them are extremely technical, and are capable of answer only by specialists. All have to do with the nature and method of revelation, rather than with the fact of revelation. I am not so much concerned as to how or through whom God gave the Bible, as I am with the fact that God gave it. It will not materially affect my faith if all of these questions of the nature and method of revelation are answered differently in the future from what they have been in the past. I only need to know that "the Bible is the book which brings to the church and to the world the true word of God concerning redemption from sin," that it is the word of God—God's book; that he has sent it forth, is behind it, has taken care of it in the past, and will throughout all time. Then I may be sure, as Professor Ladd has said in the conclusion of his discussion, "What is the Bible?" that "no discovery of modern biblical criticism, science or archeology can detract from or diminish the power of the Bible to do what God intended it should do." However, to strengthen the faith of the strong, to clarify the minds of the troubled, and to help the honest inquirer after truth, I propose to give this morning a few of the reasons why I believe the Bible to be the word of God.

1. *Unity with Diversity.*—The first reason which I mention is drawn from the fact of the wonderful unity with diversity which the Bible presents. Here we have a book, or rather, a collection of sixty-six books, written by as many as forty different authors, during a period of from 1,500 to 2,000 years. If the views of certain higher critics are to be accepted, that some of these single books were written by several authors rather than one, the force of the present argument is only made the stronger. Here, then, we have a book, or rather, a collection of sixty-six books, written by many authors during a long period of time. These writers lived and wrote in different countries, far apart from each other in space and time. Some lived and wrote under the shadow of the Pyramids in Egypt; some in the deserts of

THE BIBLE, THE WORD OF GOD

Arabia; some among the hills of Palestine; some amid the magnificence of a Nebuchadnezzar; some in the provinces of the Persians; some in the cities of Asia Minor, and Greece; some in imperial Rome. They wrote in different ages of the world. Some when the Pharaohs ruled a mightly empire upon the Nile; some when Solomon built the magnificent temple at Jerusalem; some when the proud Assyrian roamed over the plains of Mesopotamia; some when the Cæsars ruled the world. They wrote in different languages; some in the language of faith, the stately Hebrew; others in degenerate Aramaic, and others in the flowing, expressive tongue of the Greeks. They wrote in different forms of literature—we have prose and poetry, history, biography, legislation, and philosophy, orations, hymns, letters, didactic, lyric, narrative, illustrative, dramatic, and allegorical forms of literature. These writers came from different ranks in life, and represented every class in society—kings and fishermen, shepherds and statesmen, royal Isaiah, and herdsman Amos, rich and poor, uneducated and learned, prophet, priest and king, warrior, farmer, and tent-maker, royal cup bearer and regal monarch, the rough ascetic of the desert, and the polished companion at the king's court; men widely different in education and natural ability, under widely different political, social, and religious conditions, writing from their own national or temporal point of view, in their own way, with characteristic styles, peculiar phrases and constructions, and marked individuality. They treated of many different themes, of angels and demons, of earth, heaven and hell, of justice and mercy, of love and wrath, of law human and divine, of duty and destiny, of present, past, and future, of soul and body, of the individual, the family, the state; treating of or touching upon well-nigh every theme of human thought. Such is the marvelous diversity in place, time, language, literature, men, style, and themes in the Bible; and yet, amid all this diversity, there is such a unity in aim, such a oneness in all the parts, such a consistency in teaching concerning God and man, sin and salvation, and the other mighty themes which are treated, that the sixty-six books have been bound together under a common cover, and called, pre-eminently, "The Book." There is something in these books so unique as to bind them one to another, and forever to separate them from other writings. Men have tried again and again to produce other sacred writings, but the natural and the artificial flowers are separated by an immeasurable distance. There is a life, a power, a fragrance, in these writings not found elsewhere. But these books are characterized not only by a strange unity—one doctrine of God, of sin, of salvation, of heaven, of hell, of duty, which seems very remarkable—but also, from the first to the last, there is "a gradual progressiveness in the unfolding of truth; there is a steady march onward from outward and material to inward and spiritual conceptions of religion, a constantly rising and hopeful outstretching toward a better and higher future," a converging of all things toward one event, and an unfolding from that event.

Again, the uniform silence of these books upon topics which merely gratify curiosity, and the bending of all energy in discussing God's claim upon men, is a striking feature of unity. Some one has truly said, "Throughout the Bible the crimson cord of sacrifice is clearly manifest, on which the books are strung together as beads on a thread." No other collection could be made of books written at such widely separated times and places, by such different men, under such a variety of circumstances, even upon a single theme, that would manifest any such unity of thought and purpose. Only one rational explanation can be given to account for this unity amid such diversity. The Book must have been the product of one mind that planned and directed the whole of it from beginning to end, and that one mind could have been none other than God. I am told that, when the great cantilever bridge over the Niagara rapids was constructed, the various parts were made in different portions of the land, and all finished and shipped to Niagara ready for use.

They were then fastened together, and every brace and bolt and beam was an exact fit. Only one rational explanation can be given—one master mind had furnished the plans and specifications, and the several parts had been made according to the patterns given. And so this Book, written by men in different lands and times, in different languages and forms, is a unit from beginning to end, formed according to the directions of the master mind of its divine architect—God.

2. *Universal Adaptation to Human Needs.*—A second reason why I believe the Bible is the word of God is because of its universal adaptation to human needs. It is the only universal book. Other books are limited more or less to small circles of readers. Some are interesting to boys and men, others to girls and women; some are profitable to youth, others to middle life and old age; some we pick up in our joy, others we turn to in times of sadness; some are the delight of the rich and prosperous, others are the solace of the poor and the afflicted; some are favorites in the Orient, others are popular only among Anglo-Saxons. But in the Bible we find the one book of universal adaptation, suited to the needs of man and woman, old and young, rich and poor, educated and uneducated; a book not limited by clime or condition, age or nationality, into which men and women, boys and girls, of

every people, of every tongue, may look as into a mirror, and see reflected there their own needs and defects, and in which may be found a balm for every wound. This book touches life at so many points, is so adapted to every human need, that strangers, reading it for the first time, are so impressed with its truthfulness as to feel that it must have been written specially for them.* When Dr. Chambers had read to the natives of an East Indian city the first chapter of Romans, an intelligent Brahmin said to him: "Sir, that chapter must have been written for us Hindoos. It fits us exactly." In Lyons, France, an ignorant listener said to Dr. McCall, as he read the Bible to him, "Never in my life have I heard the truth so explained; my conscience answers to it." A prisoner in a Massachusetts prison, when asked why he believed the Bible to be the word of God, said, "It strikes a fellow so." This universality of the Bible makes it the most easy of all books to translate into other tongues. Of Bible translation, some one has truly said: "From Greenland to Patagonia, in the western hemisphere, and from Iceland through Europe and Asia to the Japanese and Australians, from the Copts of Egypt to the Kaffirs of South Africa, from the South Sea Islands of the Pacific through the ocean to Madagascar, the Bible has been rendered into

---

* The author here wishes to acknowledge a debt to Dr. C. H. Parkhurst for thoughts and quotations.

each language with triumphant success." Hallam, the historian, said, "I see that the Bible fits into every fold and crevice of the human heart. I am a man, and I believe that this is God's book because it is man's book." It is greater than any and every man. It is the book for the whole human race, and is destined to become so more and more. It speaks from God to the human soul. It penetrates to the innermost recesses of man's being, and satisfies the deepest yearnings of his nature. It is, as it claims to be, "living and active and sharper than any two-edged sword, and piercing even to the dividing of soul and spirit, of both joints and marrow, and quick to discern the thoughts and intents of the heart." It finds a man. It appeals to intellect, imagination and the sensibilities. The race and every individual needs redemption from sin, needs cleansing and stimulating. As long as the present order continues, there will be sin and sorrow, loneliness and death, for which no other book than the Bible can furnish a true antidote. Its universal adaptation to human needs reveals the wisdom of its author, and proves it to be divine.

3. *Its Permanence.*—A third reason why I believe the Bible is the word of God is based upon its permanence, the way in which it has survived the opposition of its foes and the abuses of its friends. What a history it has had! Through what fire and water and blood it has

THE BIBLE, THE WORD OF GOD

passed! No other book has ever been so hated by bad men, and so abused by good men. It has been put under the ban of excommunication, has been criticised and ridiculed and burnt. Every possible resource of diabolic wrath has been exhausted in the attempt to destroy it, and yet it has gone marching steadily on. Every century has produced its quota of opponents; school after school of destructive criticism has arisen, each boasting of some new discovery, or the finding of some fatal flaw, that would destroy its power. But the critics pass away, their dogmatic assertions are proved fallacious, and the grand old book gains added might. And oh! how it has been abused by its supposed friends! It has been mistranslated and misapplied. It has been worshiped as an idol and consulted as an oracle. Its sayings have been wrested from context and used to prove well-nigh everything. It has been used as authority for slavery and polygamy, has been made to sanction an inquisition and the burning of witches, to support the subjugation of women and the divine right of kings. Scarcely any freak of fanaticism, any ism or ology, has arisen in Christian lands which has not sought justification in the Bible. And yet, in spite of such terrible opposition, and such fearful handicaps, the Bible stands to-day peerless in its power and majestic in its might.

The size of a force may be estimated by the

amount of its resistance, and the real worth of a thing by its fitness to survive, and when we try to estimate the forces which have been hurled against the Bible and which have been successfully resisted, we feel that it must have behind it the very dynamite of God; and, when we consider how it has survived the centuries amid such unfavorable surroundings, we feel convinced that it is because it is best fitted to survive. Not only has it survived the actions of foes and friends, but it keeps pace with all of the discoveries of science, history, and archeology. Newly discovered monuments and manuscripts, the researches of archeology and the discoveries of science only confirm its teachings, illumine its records and give new meaning and added applications to its truths.

4. *Its Past Influence and Present Power.*—A fourth reason why I believe the Bible is the word of God is based upon its past influence and its present power. Its past influence began with the earliest times, for the Bible contains the oldest literature extant. Some of its records were doubtless written one thousand years before Herodotus, the so-called father of history, was born. Hebrew legislation is at least seven hundred years older than the laws of Lycurgus; the lyric poetry of the Bible was in its golden age nine hundred years before Horace wrote his odes; the Proverbs of Solomon are fully eight hundred years older than the treatises of Seneca,

while the book of Job probably antedated Homer by eight centuries. Of the Bible it may be said, as Napoleon said to his army at the Pyramids, "Forty centuries look down upon you." And yet, during this long period of varied experiences, the Bible has triumphantly met the supreme test. "By their fruits ye shall know them." The influence of the Bible, wherever it has had largest and longest sway, has ever been productive of the highest results. It has always been the handmaid of progress. Froude, the historian, says of the influence of the Bible in human affairs, "All that we call modern civilization in a sense which deserves the name, is the visible expression of the transforming power of the gospel." Victoria, when asked the secret of England's national strength, pointed to the Bible and said: "This is the secret of the greatness of England." Of the power of the Bible in literature, Prof. Austin Phelps says: "The Bible is to a large extent incorporated in all of the living literature of the world; not in all in equal degrees, but in all sufficiently to be felt as power. The debt of literature to the Bible is like that of vegetation to light. The hymnology of all modern languages has been absolutely created by Hebrew Psalmody. The ancient classics, so far as I know, have not contributed a single stanza to it." The greatest of modern orators also have been inspired by the Bible. The Earl of Chatham, Patrick Henry, and

Daniel Webster constantly acknowledged their debt to its pages. Art has been revolutionized, and the dissolute Venus displaced by the Divine Madonna. The Bible has always had "the singular power of attracting to itself, as friend or foe, the thinkers of the world wherever it has gone. It, with the literature commenting upon it, is more voluminous than all that remains to us of Greek and Latin literature combined. The commentaries upon the Bible exceed 60,000 volumes, while the sermons of a single year would probably amount to more than 100,000,000 octavo pages." Yet this oldest of all printed books, which for centuries has wielded such a mighty influence, is to-day the freshest, most up-to-date, most widely circulated and most largely read of all books. He who says the Bible is out of date, or is losing its power, is either ignorant on the subject, or dishonest, or both. It never has been read and studied by as many people as to-day. It has a larger circulation than any other book in the world, and "Pilgrim's Progress," which is so largely a paraphrase of Scripture, comes second. A few cold facts from only one or two of the many large Bible publishing houses will make the force of this statement more apparent. Three presses in England alone printed last year 6,000,000 Bibles and parts of Bibles for Christian worship in 320 different languages, to go to all parts of the world, to say nothing of presses in America and other lands. The daily output of the Oxford press is 4,000 Bibles, an average of 20,000 per week, or 1,000,000 each year. The weekly shipment to America of Oxford Bibles is five and one-half tons, and the demand is increasing. In the last twenty years, the demand for the Oxford Bible has doubled—500,000 copies issued in 1875, and 1,000,000 a year in 1896. The books of the British & Foreign Bible Society show likewise a marked yearly increase, 4,000,000 Bibles or portions of Bibles having been issued in one year, 1896. This one society, during the ninety-two years of its existence, has issued 147,000,000 copies of the Bible. These undeniable facts are evidence enough of the present power of the book, and of the fact that never before in its history have its teachings been so earnestly and largely studied. These four things, then, I present as some of the reasons why I believe the Bible to be the word of God—its wonderful unity with diversity, its universal adaptation to the needs of the race, its permanence in surviving the actions of foes and friends, and the advances of science and discoveries of archeology, and its past influence and present power. These four lines of evidence must amount to a demonstration to any candid mind, and bring the conviction that the Bible is none other than the word of God. No other cause is adequate to account for the effect. And yet there are in the soul of every believer still stronger reasons for the abiding conviction that the Bible is the very word of God. The surest knowledge of the deepest realities comes from self-consciousness and personal experience— knowledge which cannot be expressed in syllogistic form. Mr. Huxley has told us that "the higher truths of life are within the reach of the æsthetic faculties only"; heart wisdom is safer than head wisdom, and life mightier than logic. And the best way, after all, to be convinced of the divine origin of the Bible, is to take it and try it; make it one's counselor and guide, and test it oneself by its fruits. "If any man willeth to do his will, he shall know of the teaching, whether it be of God or whether I speak of myself." Obey and you shall know; obedience is the organ of spiritual vision. If you will take the Bible and apply it to your life faithfully and fervently, you will find that it not only gives the very highest conceptions of life and truth, but also furnishes effective motive power to urge you on to these higher realities. The more intelligently, constantly and devoutly you use it, the higher will be the product; it will transform and build up; it will draw you Godward, and in doing so will convince you that it comes from God. And when others are inclined to criticise its sacred pages, or doubt its authority, you may well say, "If you take from me this book you must give me something better, something that will do more to bless our homes, urge society, develop strength and sweetness of character, bring into human hearts love, peace, joy, long-suffering, gentleness, meekness, faith, temperance, will lessen the sorrows of life and lighten the tomb. Until you do this I shall hold to the book. I have absolute confidence in its being divine. It is the word of God. I know it through reason. I feel it in my heart, and no fires or storms can overthrow its power." Some one has thus spoken of the triumph of the Bible:

> "Last eve I paused beside a blacksmith's door,
>   And heard the anvil ring the vesper chime;
> Then, looking in, I saw upon the floor
>   Old hammers worn with beating years of time.
>
> 'How many anvils have you had?' said I,
>   'To wear and batter all those hammers so?'
> 'Just one,' said he; then said with twinkling eye,
>   'The anvil wears the hammers out, you know.'
> And so I thought the anvil of God's Word
>   For ages skeptic blows have beat upon;
> Yet, though the noise of falling blows was heard,
>   The anvil is unharmed, the hammers gone."

The Dignity and Destiny of Man

Hebrews 2:5-9.—"*For not unto the angels did he subject the world to come whereof we speak. But one hath somewhere testified, saying,*

'What is man, that thou art mindful of him?
Or the son of man, that thou visitest him?
Thou madest him a little lower than the angels;
Thou crownedst him with glory and honor,
And didst set him over the work of thy hands:
Thou didst put all things in subjection under his feet.'

For in that he subjected all things unto him, he left nothing that is not subject to him. But now we see not yet all things subjected to him. But we behold him who hath been made a little lower than the angels, even Jesus, because of the suffering of death crowned with glory and honor, that by the grace of God he should taste death for every man."

THE quotation beginning "What is man," etc., is taken from the eighth psalm. This psalm is one of the four psalms of David, expressive of his feelings as a shepherd boy, the nineteenth, twenty-third, and twenty-ninth being the other psalms of his poetical youth.

DIGNITY AND DESTINY OF MAN

This eighth psalm is a song of the night. The sun, which went forth in the morning, "as a bridegroom out of his chamber, rejoicing as a strong man to run a race," has now finished his circuit from one end of the heavens to the other, and has dropped out of sight, apparently beneath the waves of the blue Mediterranean. But no sooner does the sun disappear than the moon and the stars begin to shine. As the shades of night deepen, the stars seem to glow with greater brilliancy, and hang like balls of fire in the clear vault of an oriental sky. Those who have spent nights in Colorado recall how near and how large the stars seem to be in such an atmosphere. David is tending his father's flock on the quiet hills of Bethlehem. Being both an oriental and a shepherd poet, he is much given to star-gazing. Amid his lowly duties he has lofty thoughts. His poetic soul is aglow with inspiration. The glories of the night-time feed the muse's fire; and, as he lies upon his back amidst his sheep, and peers into the starry heavens, his soul bursts forth into ecstasy as in this eighth psalm:

"O Lord, our Lord,
How excellent is thy name in all the earth!
Who hast set thy glory upon the heavens.
Out of the mouth of babes and sucklings" (David is a mere
    boy) "hast thou established strength,
Because of thine adversaries,
That thou mightest still the enemy and the avenger.

When I consider thy heavens, the work of thy fingers,
The moon and the stars, which thou hast ordained;
What is man," (man in his weakness and littleness) "that thou art mindful of him?
And the son of man that thou visitest him?"

When I think of the heavens and their wide extent, thy creation; when I look at the moon and the countless stars, the work of thy fingers, what is weak, little, insignificant man that thy mind is full of him; and the son of man that thou art willing to visit him. This is the inspiring thought that swelled the soul of the shepherd boy. And yet, how little it was that David knew concerning the extent of God's universe! What a small world it was in which David moved! What did he know about moon or stars or heavens! What did he know about the movement of the spheres, or of countless worlds revolving about a central sun! To David, the earth was but a flat plain, more or less limited in extent; and the heavens were a tent stretched above the earth, in which moon and stars were hung as lamps. David knew nothing of the discoveries of Copernicus. David had never looked through a mighty, modern telescope, and had little conception of the vast distances to the stars. Had he possessed even one-tenth of the knowledge of one of our common-school boys or girls of to-day, with what added reverence his glowing soul would have sung:

DIGNITY AND DESTINY OF MAN

"When I consider thy heavens, the work of thy fingers,
The moon and the stars, which thou hast ordained;
What is man, that thou art mindful of him?
And the son of man, that thou visitest him?"

Evidently, bigness is not greatness, and size is not always significant. Evidently, persons are of more value than things; and men and women into whom God has breathed the breath of his own life are of more importance to him than countless worlds, the cunning workmanship of his fingers. A personal God is supremely interested in persons. Surely children in his own image and likeness are more precious than moon and stars. It is of them that his mind is full; upon them his heart is set; with them he yearns to dwell.

"For thou hast made him but little lower than the angels,
And crownest him with glory and honor.
Thou madest him to have dominion over the works of thy hands;
Thou hast put all things under his feet."

Here David recalls how, in that wonderful poem of creation, the first chapter of Genesis, it was recorded: "And God said, Let us make man in our own image, after our likeness: and let them have dominion over the fish of the sea and over the fowl of the air," etc., etc., "and over all the earth." And so David sings, in echo of the first chapter of Genesis, of the dignity and destiny of man:

"Thou madest him to have dominion over the works of thy hands;
Thou hast put all things under his feet:
All sheep and oxen" (David was even now a shepherd ruling over sheep),
"Yea, and the beasts of the field" (perhaps David recalls how he bearded the lion and slew the bear);
"The fowl of the air, and the fish of the sea,
Whatsoever passes through the paths of the seas.
O Lord, our Lord,
How excellent is thy name in all the earth!"

This is the eighth psalm, from which the writer of Hebrews quotes in this passage which I have taken as a text, and upon this quotation he now proceeds to comment. God did make man to have dominion. God did put all things in subjection under his feet. "For in that he subjected all things unto him, he left nothing that is not subject to him." Yes, man was made to have dominion, and to rule over all created things. So says the Scripture. But, as we look about upon men and the condition of things to-day, we don't see men rulers over all things. We see them not rulers, not conquerors, not masters; but in many instances and in many particulars, cringing slaves; slaves of fear, slaves of appetite and passion; slaves in body, mind and spirit. Truly, as the writer of Hebrews says, "but now we see not yet all things subjected to him." A sad sight it is, indeed, to see men and women, created in the image of God, created to have dominion, and yet not even masters of themselves. To see them slaves of self, slaves of sin, slaves of their fellows. "But now we see not yet all things subject to him. But we behold him who hath been made a little lower than the angels, even Jesus, because of the suffering of death, crowned with glory and honor, that by the grace of God he should taste death for every man." While the race in general has fallen far short of its high dignity and destiny, one man of the race, Jesus of Nazareth, has risen to the height of man's privilege and prerogative, has triumphed where others failed, and now sits crowned with glory and honor, the victorious representative of all those who through him shall also overcome. This passage, then, suggests three thoughts for our present consideration:* Man as God made him, man as sin has made him, and man as manhood was revealed in Jesus of Nazareth, and as man may become through faith in him.

1. Let us look at *the man that God made*. The first two chapters of Genesis give us a picture of man as he was created. A world of beauty and harmony was made, and at the end of each period of creation God saw that it was good. Creation proceeded on an ever ascending scale, from lower to higher, from the simple to the complex, from vegetable to lower animals, from creepers to quadrupeds. At each step God was pleased with the work of his hands. Finally, when all things

---
* *Cf.* F. B. Meyer on Hebrews *in loco*.

had been made ready to serve and minister to him, man, the climax, the masterpiece of God, was formed and established as ruler over all. "And God created man in his own image, in the image of God created he him: male and female created he them. And God blessed them: and God said unto them, 'Be fruitful, and multiply, and replenish the earth, and subdue it; and have dominion.'" Thus was man created in God's own image, and appointed to rule over the earth in God's stead. In what did this divine image and likeness consist? Doubtless it consisted in natural likeness to God, or the possession of personality; and in moral likeness to God, or the possession of holiness. Man was constituted a personal creature and a holy person. He was given certain faculties, intellect, affection, will; and these faculties were given a holy direction or tendency. By his personality, man was enabled to know himself as related to the world and to God, and was given the power to choose moral ends and to determine his purposes in life. By his holiness, or moral likeness to God, "man was created with such a direction" (trend or tendency) "of his affections and will" as to make it natural, spontaneous, for him to love and serve God. Yet, with his holiness, he retained his personal freedom, had the power of contrary choice, and was liable to temptation, even as was the second Adam, the Christ of Nazareth. Thus, in personality and holiness, in nature and in morality, was man created in the image and likeness of God. "And God said, 'Be fruitful, and multiply, and replenish the earth, and subdue it; and have dominion.'" Man was not only made in God's image, but also he was created to rule. He was constituted a king by divine right. He was God's own son, God's representative, God's vicegerent upon earth. "The sun to labor for him as a very Hercules, the moon to light his nights," and lead ocean's waters round the earth with cleansing tides, "the elements of nature to be his slaves and messengers, flowers to scent his path, fruits to please his taste, birds to sing for him, fish to feed him, beasts to toil for and carry him." Truly, his dignity and his destiny was an high one. No other book gives us such an exalted and lofty conception of man as does the Bible, and yet, no other book paints so truly and vividly the deceitfulness and depravity of the unrenewed heart. The idolater regards himself as inferior to beasts and birds and crawling things, and bows in reverence to worship them. The materialist thinks himself only flesh and blood, a mass of matter formed by the chance accumulation of unreasoning atoms. Some so-called scientists regard man as the offspring of the monkey, and feel rather sure that they can trace their own ancestry back to the brute. But the Bible, with its true conception of man as well as of God, rises above all of these misrepresentations, and boldly declares man to be the child of a heavenly Father, created in his image and after his likeness. Thus we behold the man that God made, in a world of beauty, harmony and peace, in which he himself is "lord of all he surveys." He is surrounded with a magnificent palace yard, the garden of Eden. He walks and talks with God in the most familiar way. His employment is of the most delightful kind, for God loves him too much to doom him to idleness. He is to trim the trees, train the flowers, and gather the fruits of the garden. His dominion is boundless. His rule is absolute. He is king over all things. Nevertheless, there is one limitation of his power, one condition of his reign. His will must be subordinate to the will of the Almighty. He must bow down and worship the God who made him. This, for a time, the man seemed willing to do; and so long as he did so, he retained his almost sovereign sway. But now, tempted by a rebel to distrust God's love and God's wisdom, man became uneasy under the sole limitation of his power. Ambition was aroused; and, when promised that upon one act of disobedience his eyes should be opened, and he should become equal with God, man voluntarily stepped over the mark, raised his own will in rebellion against his Maker's, broke away from communion with his Father, and lost his crown.

2. This brings us secondly to the beginning of

that sad history of *man as sin has made him*. No sooner does man sin than conscience makes him a coward. Yonder is that erstwhile sovereign man, hiding like a cringing slave "behind the trees of the garden from the Lord of the garden." He is now no longer king. He has dethroned himself. His crown is rolling in the dust. Selfishness has now become the supreme rule of existence; the soul has lost communion with the source of its life; the holy nature has become tainted and perverted; affections are corrupted, intellect blinded, will fettered. Now he finds it easier to sin than to do right, for self has become his God. He has begun the downward path, and down, down, down, he goes, at a terrific rate. Fallen man begets children in his own fallen likeness, and hands down his corrupted nature and perverted disposition to his descendants. Fear, jealousy, hate, soon take possession of man, and the deteriorating process is hastened by his own multiplied and multiplying sins. Cain kills Abel, and his sin reacts upon himself and still further debases his own character. So low does man become, so much a slave of his guilty self, that we soon see this one-time monarch, this one made for dominion, bowing down in worship before the weakest and lowest creatures of his kingdom. Yonder, in Egypt, he worships frogs, and flies, and pays homage to serpents. Here he has consecrated a temple to the sacred bull, while yonder he kisses the dust in reverence before a golden calf. He trembles as a suppliant before "sticks and stones and worse than senseless things." Or, to-day, he is a slave of fear and remorse, of appetite and passion, of drinks and drugs, of society and custom. The image of God, in which he was created, has not been lost; but it is sadly marred and scarred by sin and selfishness. Man is a lost sheep, afar off on the mountains, away from the shepherd's fold. He is a lost coin, still valuable, stamped with the image and superscription of a king; but lost to its highest usefulness and missing the very purpose of its existence. He is a lost son; still a son of his Father, but a prodigal, his will in rebellion against his Father's will, and his life deprived of the blessings and privileges of the home-life. Yes, he is lost, *lost*, LOST! Nevertheless, he is capable of redemption; for he still possesses personality and a moral nature, however much that moral nature may have been perverted. Yes, man, a failure, may yet become man, a success. Paradise Lost may yet be Paradise Regained. "For the Son of Man came to seek and to save those that are lost." Christ came not only to reveal to us the Father, but to reveal us to ourselves. He came to show us what manhood meant; what man might have been; and what a man, through him, may yet become.

3. Let us note then, thirdly, *man as Christ revealed manhood*, manhood to which we also may

DIGNITY AND DESTINY OF MAN 123

attain through faith in him. In Christ manhood was at its maximum, and the ancient ideal was fully realized in every particular. He was preeminently *the man*, the Son of Man, the perfect man; the only member of the human race in whom has been manifested the complete idea of humanity. He must forever stand at the very apex of mankind. No improvement can ever be made upon him. In him, we find every virtue carried to its highest excellence; in him, we find no vice, even in its lightest form. The verdict of all who carefully scrutinize his character must be but a re-echoing of the judgment of Pilate, "I find no fault in him." You may take any other very good man, with the most distinguished heredity, with the strongest and sweetest character, with the most auspicious environment, and, through the education of life, books and communion with God and man, you may develop him, through centuries, to the very highest point of excellence, and in this wonderful man you'll not find any virtue, any excellence of character, that you do not find in the man of Galilee. Christ possessed and combined, in the most remarkable way, "every grace and every virtue which human nature ever has displayed, or ever will display, in the course of its universal development. Matchless beauty, spotless purity, stainless splendor, strength with gentleness, courage with tenderness, charity with righteousness"; the lowliest and yet the lordliest, the meekest and yet the mightiest of men. He realized in his life what the first Adam and his descendants, through sin, failed to realize. He manifested God's image and God's likeness everywhere. He was sovereign in all his commands. He was king over himself, over nature, over all created things. Winds and waves obeyed him. "Trees withered at his touch." Fish in shoals came at his call. Droves of cattle fled before his scourging whip. Disease, demons and death bowed before his will. In every way he trod the earth as a conqueror; and now, as victorious man, as well as Son of God, he sits crowned with glory and honor. The first man, Adam, believed the lie of the devil, and lost his crown. The second man, Christ, obeyed at every point the will of his Father, and now sits enthroned in his glorified humanity. The first man, Adam, aspired, through disobedience, to equality with God, and lost his earthly kingdom. The second man, Christ, stooped down from a heavenly throne, took upon himself humanity, partook of flesh and blood, lived a perfect and obedient life as a Son, as a man, and now, as man's representative, he sits crowned. As Paul tells us in Philippians, "being found in fashion as a man, he humbled himself and became obedient unto death, even the death of the cross; wherefore God hath highly exalted him."

Yes, Christ has triumphed, and is crowned; but

only as a first fruits, as the captain of our salvation, as the leader "of many sons to glory," as the "first among many brethren." He, the victorious man, offers to help us win a similar victory. "As many as received him, to them gave he the power" (the right) "to become the sons of God, even to them that believe on his name." There is only one way by which the dignity and destiny of man may again be realized, and that is through faith in him. If we join our lives with his, and let him live in and through us, we shall surely win. We shall be "more than conquerors through him that loved us." Through fellowship with him, it may be true of each one of us, that there is no sin or sinful tendency which we may not overcome, and no virtue or excellence to which we may not attain. The progress may seem slow, and the attainment distant. We shall need to exercise patience with ourselves, and patience with each other, but the outcome cannot be doubtful. The main thing now is, are you tending in the right direction? Is your life a victorious life? Are you becoming more and more like your Master? Which is it in your case, conqueror or conquered? Victor or victim? Is the life getting sweeter, the character stronger; are the purposes higher? If so, then take courage; for through him you shall surely conquer. You shall see him as he is. Yes, you shall be like him.

And is there some one here this evening who is living without the conscious help of such a Savior? One who feels himself being more and more overcome; who realizes that the divine image and likeness have been sadly scarred and soiled by sin and selfishness? Will you not give up your own unaided and vain efforts after truest manhood or womanhood, and take Christ as your best helper and friend? He knows all of your trials. He is thoroughly fitted to be your Savior. He has been tempted in all points as you, and has triumphed. Accept him as your Savior now, and you'll begin at once to overcome. You must stoop to conquer, but he will crown you at the last. The possibilities of a life have been illustrated by the history of a silk rag. Yonder is a rag-picker, going up and down the streets and lanes of the city, picking up rags and pieces of paper, which she carelessly thrusts into a dirty-looking bag. Thus she spends many weary hours of the day. But now, she sees something which specially arouses her interest. It's soiled and dirty, and half buried in an ash heap. It looks like the commonest sort of a cast-off rag. But she picks it up, with the greatest interest, carefully smoothes it over her knee, and, instead of thrusting it carelessly into the junk-bag, she carefully puts it into her pocket. It isn't worth much. It's only a dirty rag; *but it's silk!* The rag-picker takes it to the broker and gets perhaps a penny for it; the broker sends it to the renovator; the renovator sends it, with other silk rags, to the paper mills at Eau Claire, where the finest of fine paper is made from it. It's now worth perhaps fifteen cents. Then the government sends to Eau Claire an order for some extra fine paper; the paper is sent on to Washington, and is stamped, and the old rag now becomes a government bond of immense worth. *The rag was silk!* So, my friend, if you'll give your soiled and scarred life into the hands of the world's great Redeemer, he'll purge you from your impurities, he'll renew your heart, he'll lead you, develop you, train you and enlarge you through time and throughout eternity, until there shall be no virtue which you shall not realize, and no height which you may not reach. May God help each one of us, through Christ, to attain here and hereafter to the true dignity and destiny of manhood and womanhood.

Sorrows Sanctified

James 1:2-4.—"*My brethren, count it all joy when ye fall into divers temptations; knowing this, that the trying of your faith worketh patience. But let patience have her perfect work, that ye may be perfect and entire, wanting nothing.*"

THE epistle in which the words of our text are found was written by that James, the brother of our Lord, who was for years at the head of the Jerusalem church. It was addressed to the Christian Jews, who were at this time scattered over the entire known world; and it had as its purpose their comfort and admonition in view of existing and future trials. The lot of the Christian Jew was indeed a hard one, and it was very appropriate that some such words as those of our text should have been written to him, to buoy him up in the midst of his overwhelming woes.

His troubles came, in general, from two sources. There were, first, the unchristian Jews, that vast majority of the Jewish nation, who still clung tenaciously to Judaism, and had nought but curses and revilings for any who espoused the cause of the hated Nazarene. If, perchance, any one of their own number renounced Judaism for Christianity, he was earnestly labored with, and all possible efforts were made to reclaim him from the error of his ways. It is probable that many were thus induced to return to Judaism, since the book to the Hebrews was called forth to counteract just such a tendency. If, however, a Jew persisted in his new-born faith, he was considered a breeder of disorder, a heretic; was subjected to the most bitter denunciations; was mercilessly dragged before the synagogue for trial; and, as history seems to show, sometimes received sentence of death. The bitterness of these persecutions was still sharpened, when one's persecutors were those of one's own home, one's own flesh and blood; when wife and father, son and daughter, vied with one another in heaping curses upon the new-born Christian and his beloved Redeemer. Oh! we at this distant day, and in these Christian times, can have little idea of the terrible hatred of which the Jew was capable. The hatred which these Jews had for their apostate brethren is well expressed by Shakespeare, when he puts into the mouth of Shylock, respecting Antonio, the words:

"I hate him, for he is a Christian.
If I can catch him once upon the hip
I will feed fat the ancient grudge I bear him."

Hatred has found its very incarnation in the Judases and Shylocks of history, and in the howling mob which thronged the throne of Pilate and only quenched its thirst in the blood of the Son of God.

But these Christian Jews, in common with all Jews, had also another source of trouble. It was the presence everywhere in their beloved land of the conquering Roman. Judea was now a Roman province; her freedom was gone; the legions of the Emperor were quartered in all her cities; the most sacred rites and places of her history were defiled by heathen bands; on all sides appeared the signs of decay and of ultimate national extinction; and within twenty years from the time of the writing of this Epistle, Jerusalem, the City of Peace, the center of the grandest, most momentous and most terrible events of Jewish, if not of the world's, history, will have been burned by the Roman, Titus.

In view of such present and future trials, the words of our text would not have failed to command careful attention. But perhaps some one may say, "These words have no reference to us, since we have no such trials as those of our early Christian brethren. Why should we give heed to such a text as this?" We answer, it is true that these words were written primarily for a certain people, under certain social, political and religious distresses; true that many of us to-day are not in similar circumstances; but we all have trials and troubles of various sorts. We all, I say, have trials and troubles. Mine are no greater than yours, and yours are no greater than mine; and these words contain principles of life so broad as to be applicable to all times and to all people, and were intended, under divine Providence, to be a source of comfort and consolation to all of God's children in every age of the world. Let us, then, consider for this morning, the theme, "Sorrows Sanctified," or, "The divine ideal of Christian conduct in the midst of trials."

It is well to recall, in passing, that the word translated in our text *temptation* does not convey to us the exact idea of the original Greek. The word *trial*, as given by the revisers in the margin, and preferred by the American Committee, is less likely to be misunderstood. By a temptation we generally mean a seduction to evil, an inclination to sin, an impulse to do that which is wrong; while the word trial is broader, and, though it contains the meaning of the word temptation, refers here also to what we call sorrows, trouble, disappointment, such as come from the loss of property, of position or reputation, of health or of friends.

Notice, again, that our text assumes the existence, not of a single trial, but of divers, many-colored trials. These Christian Jews were encompassed with trials. We have mentioned but two sources of woe. Trials are many and of various kinds, and as we read the history of the past, or reflect on the condition of things to-day, we recognize the truth of the text, and sometimes say, in a proverbial form, "Troubles never come singly."

To persons under such circumstances, in the midst of many varied trials, the words of our text come, "Count it all joy when ye fall into divers temptations."

1. We note, in the first place, that trials are largely subjective. Seneca, a famous Latin writer, said, "Our grief lieth in our own opinion and conception of miseries," while Emerson, of our own times, expressed a similar sentiment when he said, "The light in which we see the world comes from the soul of the observer." Let me illustrate the truth expressed in these rather abstract statements. Here are two men whose afflictions are in themselves equal. This, of course, is a presumptive case, for no two men have trials which are exactly similar; and yet allow the case for purposes of illustration. Here are two persons whose trials are in themselves equal. To the one they appear as crushing woes; to the other they are afflictions which endure but for a moment. The one is borne down and overcome by them; the other bears bravely up under and rises above them. The one is rendered narrow and hard-hearted, the other is broadened, developed and rendered tender-hearted. The one is marred by them, the other is made by them.

Where lies the difference? Not in the afflictions themselves, but in the attitude of the two men toward them. Compare Pharaoh and Job. The plagues of the frogs, the lice, the flies, the boils, and the darkness fell upon Pharaoh, and at the end of the story of each we read the melancholy words, "And Pharaoh's heart was hardened." Upon Job even severer afflictions fell. His oxen, his asses, his sheep, his camels, his servants, yea, all his children, were taken away; and yet, at the end of this catalogue of fatalities, we read this significant statement: "Then Job arose and rent his mantle and shaved his head and fell down upon the ground and worshiped and said, 'Naked came I out of my mother's womb, and naked shall I return thither: the Lord gave and the Lord hath taken away, blessed be the name of the Lord.'" Afflictions, then, are largely subjective, and much depends upon the attitude of men toward them.

2. Again, the nature of man's endurance of trial, as well as the effect of trial upon his character, depends upon his belief, his faith in respect to two things: First, what is the source and immediate purpose of affliction? As regards this question, men can be divided into two great classes. There are, of course, all shades of belief, but these two classes will be found to be fairly representative. In the days of Greek philosophers, the Stoics were a large and influential

school. They held that the universe was nothing but the expression of a blind, unintelligent force. Joys and sorrows come alike to all. A blind fate determines all of the events of life. There is no purpose in events. There is no philosophy of life, except the philosophy of cold, stoical endurance. Man is a machine, a puppet in a show, a thing without volition, irresistibly driven on to a purposeless destiny by an impersonal and remorseless Fate. Personality? There is none in God or man.

The Stoic, in the midst of affliction, contracted his features, gritted his teeth, folded his arms, firmly placed his heel on the ground, and said, "I endure because I must." There was no cheer, no uplift, no joy, no buoyancy, about such an endurance as that. It was purely animal courage, hardly worthy even of admiration. The American Indian was a fine modern example of the ancient Stoic. It is needless to remark that to-day there is a large number of people whose system of thought and manner of life are fatalistic and stoical in their tendency.

In striking contrast with this class of men stands a class of persons whom we call Christians. The Christian believes in a personal God, a God all-powerful, yet all-wise, holy, yet benevolent, a being who desires the highest good of every one of his creatures. The Christian believes, and here I would not be misunderstood, that all trials and afflictions of every sort come directly or indirectly under the providing or permitting providence of a personal, holy and benevolent God, and that they are disciplinary in their purpose; that they are a test of faith, and that God, as a wise father, chastens (trains) whom he loves. In view of this fact, these Jewish Christians and all followers of the meek and lowly Jesus are urged to be cheerful in the midst of various trials, knowing this, that the trying of their faith worketh patience, or, rather, endurance. For one, who professes to be a believer in God and a follower of the patient and suffering Savior, to be a discontented grumbler, a kicker, a morose complainer and a pessimistic bore, is to impugn the character of God, to cast reflections on the truth of his Word, to disgrace the Church of Christ, and to help to make the name of Christian a byword and a reproach. As you believe in God and his eternal purpose, as you believe in Christ and his saving power, as you believe in the Holy Spirit and his ministrations of comfort and peace, as you profess to have your life hidden with Christ in God, and to be walking by faith in him, as seeing him who is invisible, in the name of the Triune God, I beseech of you:

> "Look up and not down;
> Look out and not in;
> Look forward and not back
> And lend a hand."

A faith which has never been tested is generally a weak, sickly sort of thing. The house-plant which has been carefully guarded from all opposing winds and currents, the hot-house flowers which have been ever accustomed to a constant temperature, quickly wither and fall away when the hoar-frost strikes them; but that sapling, faith, which stands out in the open field, where winds and storms play upon it, sends its shoots deeper at every tug of the tempest, and wreathes its roots around the everlasting rocks. It's when we have to buffet the storm, when the tempests roar, and the earth trembles beneath our feet, that faith is tested, and through testing becomes firm. Out of struggle strength is born, and from the midst of conflict convictions come. No one realizes the trustworthiness of God, or the faithfulness of his promises, as he who has been through the furnace of trouble and found them true. Such an one feels sure that "all things work together for good to those that love God."

"The trying of faith worketh patience." How shall we describe this marvelous product, patience! They call it a negative virtue, a silent virtue, a passive virtue; but if it is negative and silent and passive, it is not less powerful. The mightiest forces of the universe are the silent forces.

> "The heavens declare the glory of God
> And the firmament showeth his handiwork.

SORROWS SANCTIFIED

> Day unto day uttereth speech
> And night unto night sheweth knowledge.
> There is no speech nor language
> Their voice is not heard.
> Their line is gone out through all the earth
> And their words to the end of the world."

The power that whirls the worlds through space is noiseless, but it is none the less resistless. We speak, to be sure, of the music of the spheres, but it is a symphony of silence. "Worketh patience." This wonderful product is not produced in a moment. If patience is so great a power and so excellent a virtue, it is worth the winning. It is not to be acquired by spasmodic fits of endeavor; but little by little, as day by day we faithfully do life's duties.

> "Heaven is not reached by a single bound,
> But we build the ladder by which we rise
> From the lowly earth to the vaulted skies,
> And we mount to its summit round by round."

3. Again, the nature of man's conduct under trial, and the effect of trial upon him, depend upon his faith in the end of his trials, or in their ultimate purpose. "Knowing this, that the trying of your faith worketh patience; but let patience have her perfect work, that ye may be perfect and entire, wanting nothing." Faith in the end is the key to all the noblest endurance of history. Read the thrilling romance of discovery and invention, and you will realize that that which

sustained those hardy heroes and pioneers in travel and thought, in the midst of indescribable trials, was faith in the end. Four hundred years ago, a bold Genoese sailor, a man of great faith, set out with a few companions on a long journey upon an unknown sea. After days and weeks of varied experience, the waves rough beneath them, the clouds black above them, with nought in their horizon but heaven and ocean, his companions become discouraged and disheartened. Faces become black with anger and fear. Murmurings, silent at first, become more open and pronounced. Dark despair broods over the ship; and at last mutiny, that terror of the sea, surges in every breast. In the midst of this scene of distress stands a man, firm and erect, with cheerful countenance and hopeful mien. No clouds of despondency play over his features; but, with keen eyes and an air of expectancy, he eagerly surveys the horizon before him. How is it that he seems not to heed the trials about him? What is it that enables him to endure so bravely the experience through which he is passing? He sees before him India. His eye of faith pierces the unknown expanse, and the end of his trials he sees to be a new passage round the world. Fifty years after, go with me to France and see a man who has been working patiently for sixteen years, amid great hardships, toward the realization of an idea. His resources are now well-nigh spent.

SORROWS SANCTIFIED

His furnace fires have devoured his substance, and in his extremity he begins to split up his furniture for fuel. His neighbors mock him. His wife derides him. His starving children plead with him. Death stares all in the face. Yet we see that this man, firm as a rock, strong in his determination, and buoyant in his expectancy, is moved by none of these things. Why? Because Bernard Palissy knew that if he could keep his furnace fires hot enough, he could produce the beautiful white enamel which he was seeking. Faith in the end made endurance possible. All down through history, from the beginning of time, the character of man's endurance of trouble has depended upon his faith in the end. Abraham journeyed from Ur of Chaldee into unknown parts, sustained by his faith in the Promised Land. Job rose above the afflictions which fell upon him, and triumphed over his friends by his sublime faith in the outcome of his trials, when he exultantly declared, "I know that my Redeemer liveth." Stephen, when the stones came crashing in upon him, by faith saw Jesus and the home of the saints. Paul and Silas sang songs in the jail at Philippi. A host of martyrs welcomed the stake, bathed their hands in the flames, and joyfully endured the severest trials because of their faith in the end. Reformers and missionaries have furnished many examples of this principle. And who can doubt that one great sustaining power in the life of suffering of Jesus himself was a clear view of the final purpose of his work, the salvation of the world? Our text suggests to us the final end of all our trials, in view of which we are cheerfully and patiently to endure the troubles through which we may be called to pass. It is perfection of character. "But let patience have her perfect work, that ye may be perfect and entire, lacking in nothing." Trial in the furnace of sorrow, when borne in the right spirit, will do for human character what the fire does for precious metals; it will burn away the dross, and bring out into clearer light that which is of real worth. How often have we seen the kinks of character removed by affliction! How often we have noticed that a broadness of living, a sympathy of thought and feeling, and a tenderness and gentleness of love and behavior have been wrought into a man's disposition by the hammer of discipline! Why was it necessary for the chosen people to pass through that severe bondage in Egypt? Why those forty years of trial in the wilderness? Why that checkered history of more than a thousand years? Why that Babylonish captivity? This was God's way of building a nation. This is the divine method of bringing about perfection, both in nations and in individuals. Why is it that God so often causes us to pass through these dark valleys? Why is it that sickness strikes us down and interrupts our work; that disappointments cross our path; that many of our cherished plans are frustrated? Why? We believe that it is because God is training us. Life is a training school, and trials are our best teachers. The end of all is our highest welfare, our perfection of character. We shall acquire this in proportion as we allow patience to have her perfect work.

"Let us," then, "be patient. These severe afflictions
   Not from the ground arise;
But oftentimes celestial benedictions
   Assume this dark disguise."

Further, let us recall that we have observed that patient endurance depends upon faith in the source and immediate purpose of afflictions, and faith in the end. It is pre-eminently a work of faith. Our sight is very limited.

"We see but dimly through the mists and vapors;
   Amid these earthly damps,
What seem to us but sad, funereal tapers
   May be heaven's distant lamps."

We cannot see even a day before us, and life appears to our thoughts as made up of so many hours and minutes. We see nothing as a unit, or as a finality. We see only parts of things. Life to us is a mass of incompletions. Life is like climbing a series of ever-rising hills which lead up to a lofty mountain. We climb up the first hill, and when we have reached the top, we can see nothing before us but a dark valley and perhaps a dimly rising hillside. We can see no more. All is veiled in fog and mist. We pass down through this valley, over a mountain stream, up the hillside, and attain the second height. Here, again, before us, we can see but a short distance, and that a valley and a crooked path; but, as we look back from this vantage point, we can see the way in which we have come, and begin to understand why it was that we must cross that valley and follow that winding road. On and on we go, through valley to hill-top; and, as we trudge along, the way behind us, over which we have come, begins to take definite form, and we begin to see that there has been a constant ascent; while before us the mist is lifting, and the mountain peak toward which we are striving becomes more plain. On and on we go, now ascending, now winding down a crooked path; again we begin to rise, and at last we reach the summit of the mountain peak. The glow of the noontide sun has now burst upon us. The mists are gone; and we wonderingly admire the beauty of the scene. As we gaze here and there, our thoughts are drawn to the place of our ascent. We trace with eager curiosity the windings of the path by which we have come to this magnificent height. And now, *now*, we understand the meaning of every step. We see that each winding of the road was necessary. Such is life. We can see but a short distance before us. We pass into dark places and afflictions rise up before us and shut out the light of the world from us. A cent, when held close to the eye, appears larger than the universe. How much depends upon getting the proper point of view! Some years ago, while in a fine-art gallery in Europe, I stood one day before a famous picture. I gazed and gazed, and yet I could see no beauty there. Everything seemed to be jumbled. There was no order, no perspective, simply blotches of color. All at once the thought flashed across my mind, "Perhaps the fault is with me, and not with the picture." I stepped aside a few paces. No; it was of no use. I could find no beauty in those splashes of color. I was just about to leave the gallery, disgusted with myself and with the picture; when, as I reached the door, I turned about to take a final look. And now, behold! all seemed changed. Order had come out of disorder. Every object seemed to stand out in wonderful perspective, and before me was a scene of exquisite beauty. The picture was the same, but I had gotten the artist's point of view. Again, we have an illustration of life. When we get the divine perspective, we see things in their true relations. We often have the experience of seeing, in later years, that what we regarded at the time as a very bitter disappointment, a very hard providence, was, in fact, the greatest blessing which God could at the time have bestowed upon us. Then we realize that every cloud had a silver lining, and that our sorrows were but blessings in disguise. Dear friends, life, with its so-called accidents and exigencies, when viewed from any standpoint but the right one, seems a meaningless jumble, an insolvable problem, a purposeless series of disconnected events. But when we get the divine point of view, when our faith pierces the mists, and sees the mountain peak as our goal, when every event in life is seen to be a part, and a necessary part too, of a great plan, when perfection of character is known to be the end of our trials; then these afflictions will appear as sorrows of a moment, and our patient endurance will work in us the perfection which God desires. Then, at all times, we may sing with the sainted P. P. Bliss:

> "So on I go, not knowing,
>   I would not if I might;
> I'd rather walk in the dark with God
>   Than go alone in the light.
> I'd rather walk by faith with Him
>   Than go alone by sight.
> Where He may lead I'll follow,
>   My trust in Him repose,
> And every hour in perfect peace
>   I'll sing 'He knows, He knows,'
>   I'll sing 'He knows, He knows!'"

Change Your Mind!

Isaiah 55:7.—"*Let the wicked forsake his way, and the unrighteous man his thoughts: and let him return unto the Lord, and he will have mercy upon him; and to our God, for he will abundantly pardon.*"

Ezekiel 33:11.—"*Say unto them, as I live, saith the Lord God, I have no pleasure in the death of the wicked; but that the wicked turn from his way and live: turn ye, turn ye from your evil ways; for why will ye die, O house of Israel?*"

Matt. 4:17.—"*From that time began Jesus to preach, and to say, 'Repent ye, for the kingdom of heaven is at hand.'*"

Acts 17:30.—"*The times of ignorance, therefore, God overlooked; but now he commandeth men that they should all everywhere repent.*"

THE portions of Scripture just read are only a few of the many passages, in both the Old and the New Testaments, which insist upon the duty and doctrine of repentance. Repentance was a familiar message in biblical times; its meaning ought to be specially clear to-day. Should I ask, however, an average audience for a definition of Scriptural repentance, we should be surprised at the variety of the answers given. Many have an inadequate idea of its scope; many confound other things with it. Let us ask ourselves what it is, and what it is not. The word in the original which is translated "Repent," means literally, "To think differently after, an afterthinking, a change of mind resulting in a change of conduct." Dr. John A. Broadus, the great American New Testament Greek scholar, defined repentance as "a change of mind, thought and purpose as regards sin, and the service of God; a change naturally accompanied by deep sorrow for past sin, and naturally leading to a change of outward life." In the Old Testament the corresponding injunction is, "Turn ye, turn ye, or return." In the Latin version we have the translation "exercise penitence," which with ritualists soon came to mean "do penance." But thought is the source of deep and true feeling, and thought and feeling lead to action. The change of mind, thought, or purpose is, therefore, the primary idea; while feeling, or grief for sin, is secondary: not grief for sin first and change of mind second, as some would have us suppose. And so, when Old Testament prophet and New Testament preacher united in echoing the divine injunction, "Repent ye! Repent ye!" they were saying in nineteenth century English, "Change your mind! Change your mind!" Isaiah said it. Ezekiel said it. John the Baptist said it. Christ said it. The twelve said it. Peter said it. Paul said it. "Change your mind! Change your mind! For

CHANGE YOUR MIND!

the kingdom of God is at hand." And to-day, as a humble follower of a long line of faithful preachers of the cross, each ministering to his own generation, each proclaiming, as God's messenger, the blessed gospel of salvation, I too, in God's name, call upon you to "change your mind."

Change your mind about God. Some people think of God as a great, burly, arbitrary, despotic Being; a terrible Judge before whom we must appear; a hard Task-master trying to drive on to slavish toil a helpless and hopeless race; an awful Ogre; a Monster, lawless and loveless. But this is not the God of the Bible, nor the God of the universe. God is not a monster, but a benevolent Creator, and a loving Heavenly Father. He made man, his masterpiece, in His own image and likeness; and to rule. He created a beautiful world of harmony and peace for man's home; and when man, by his own voluntary sin, defiled his heart and home, and destroyed the bliss of earth, God did not leave him alone in his misery and woe, but came to teach him the blight of sin, and to point him forward in hope to the time of victory over evil through the woman's seed. In the fulness of time God's own Son, born of a woman, came into the world as a man, to win a victory for man; and to bring man back to fellowship with God, and into the relationship of sonship with a Heavenly Father. You must change your mind about God. God loves you. God desires you to be His son, to see in Him your Father. Yes! He loves YOU, every one of you, the very vilest and weakest, the most ungrateful and selfish of you. He has always loved you. He desires to save every one of you. "For God so loved the world that he gave his only-begotten Son, that whosoever believeth on him should not perish, but have eternal life." His supreme desire for you is that you may choose his Son as your Savior, Friend and Brother; and through Him learn how to be a child of God. For, "as many as received Him, to them gave He the right to become children of God, even to them that believe on His name." Change your mind about God now! He is your Friend. He desires your very highest welfare. He wants many sons, and wants to bring those sons to glory. He wants you to be his child. He yearns to teach you through the Spirit to cry "Abba, Father."

Then, too, you must change your mind not only about God, but also about man, about yourself. You are not a mere body; not all physical; not "a mass of matter formed by the chance accumulation of unreasoning atoms"; not simply an animal. You are something more than the brutes. You are a person. You have mental possibilities. You have a spiritual capacity. Like the temple of old, you have the outer court, the body; the inner court, the mind; and the holy of holies, the spirit. And in some of you this spiritual part of your nature, like the deserted Temple in the time of Pompey, is dark and tenantless. Oh, that you would open the door now and let the Savior in! Man is, above all things, a spiritual being, with a capacity for God; and it is impossible for him ever to find permanent peace or rest away from God. No spiritual being can ever be fully satisfied with material things; nor find his highest or fullest development in the realm of the visible. Come! Change your mind about yourself! You have divine possibilities. Your spiritual capacity is the best and most enduring thing about you. Let God into your soul and you will, indeed, begin to live.

You must change your mind also about sin. In the olden time, the Tempter led our first parents to believe that sin was a good thing, was an advantage. "And when the woman saw that the tree was good for food, and that it was a delight to the eyes, and that the tree was to be desired to make one wise, she took of the fruit thereof, and did eat; and she gave also unto her husband with her, and he did eat." And it has been thus ever since. People only sin at first under the false impression that they are going to gain something by it. Later on people sin from force of habit and strength of appetite. But at first we are led to suppose that this or that sin, this or that indulgence, will be the road to advantage. But the call of God, the message of Scripture, the verdict of history, observation and experience, the voice of wisdom, all cry out in stentorian tones, "Change your mind! Change your mind!" Sin is never a real gain. There is no permanent advantage in wrong-doing. Sin is always, as the Hebrew word describes it, a missing of the mark, a loss, a mistake. Be wise in time and forsake sin!

Again, you must change your mind about righteousness. You have thought that the path of self-indulgence and sin was the path of joy and peace; and that the path of right-doing was narrow and disappointing. You must change your mind! Righteousness does not mean compression, but expression; not slavery but highest liberty; not a burden but a boon; not a fast, nor a funeral, but a feast of good things. Satan is inducing you to live on sawdust, to feed on the pods that the swine eat. But God says, "Hearken diligently unto me, and eat ye that which is good, and let your soul delight itself in fatness." Sin always cramps and warps, dwarfs and destroys; but righteousness enlarges and develops, builds up, makes for manhood and womanhood. To be a Christian means to "have life and to have it more abundantly." Listen! There is not in Christianity a single duty or doctrine, that will dim or destroy one single honest delight of the human heart. Not one! It aims a deadly blow only at sin and selfishness. It aims to destroy that which is already destroying you. Change your mind about righteousness!

Once more; you must change your mind about Christ, the supreme figure of human history. You must change your mind about Christ. He is not a mere historical personage; one who lived and died nineteen hundred years ago, a martyr to an unfortunate series of circumstances. He is not merely the ideal man, the best man that ever lived. He is God as well as man, the God-man Christ Jesus, who, in order to provide a salvation for every member of the human race, lived and died and rose again, and lives to-day at God's right hand, where He shall sit till His enemies be made the footstool of His feet. He tasted death for every man; He was made perfectly fitted through suffering to be the captain of our salvation, yours and mine; He is not one who cannot be touched with the feeling of our infirmities, but is able to sympathize with and help us; having made a propitiation for our sins, He is ever living to make intercession for us, and so is able to save to the uttermost all those who come to God through Him. Change your mind about Christ, and accept Him now as your Savior!

This is fundamentally the call to repentance. Change your mind about God, and see in Him a Friend and Father! Change your mind about yourself, and recognize your spiritual nature and possibilities! Change your mind about sin, and see in it that which only warps and destroys! Change your mind about righteousness, and see in it fulness of life! Change your mind about Christ, and see in Him your Savior! To bring you to this change of mind God has been using, is using, and will continue to use—every possible resource within his power, without interfering with your freedom of choice. He wishes that none should perish but that all should come to the knowledge of the truth. Christ's life and death and resurrection prove God's love for you in the past; the pleading of the Holy Spirit, the presentation of truth to your soul, the presence of opportunities for you to accept Christ and be saved now, are evidence abundant of God's present love for and interest in YOU. Change your mind and turn to Him!

Repentance, then, is a change of mind, leading to a change of conduct. It is man's act, by virtue of which he puts himself in a position to accept salvation from God through Christ. It is an absolutely necessary prerequisite to salvation; not a means, or in any way meritorious, but a necessary condition of forgiveness.

If this change of mind is thorough and genuine, it will be accompanied with a change of feeling and lead to and result in a change of conduct. For true repentance involves and includes five things: (1) Conviction of sin; (2) Contrition for sin; (3) Confession of sin; (4) Turning from sin;

(5) Surrender to Christ. How much conviction must there be? Dr. Strong definitely answers, "Enough to induce the sinner promptly and persistently to turn from sin to Christ." Less than this is not enough. More than this is not necessary. There must be also sorrow for sin, and confession of sin; or there will be no turning away from sin, and turning to and accepting of Christ. Nor will confession of sin avail, unless there is a turning away from sin. Pharaoh said, "I have sinned," but went on doing the same thing the next day. Nor will turning away from sin avail, unless there is some one who can save from sin. There must be a surrender to Christ. Thus each step involves the others; and if repentance is genuine, all will be included. True repentance never exists without faith, and true faith always is accompanied by repentance.

Repentance, then, is not to be confounded with fear. In a storm on the sea certain godless men stopped their swearing, gambling and drinking, fell upon their knees and began to pray. You think it an example of repentance? Let us wait and we can determine. When the terrible storm was over, and a little time had passed, the game was soon restarted; oaths, at first moderate and less violent, soon became blasphemous; and carousing continued. You say, repentance? No! Not repentance, but fear.

Nor is repentance to be confounded with feeling. It is easy to make people cry, but not so easy to lead them to repentance. Nor is repentance to be identified with remorse. Judas had remorse, and went out and hanged himself.

> "Repentance and remorse are not the same;
> That is a heavenly, this an earthly flame:
> One springs from love, and is a welcome guest;
> And one an iron tyrant o'er the breast.
> Repentance weeps before the crucified;
> Remorse is nothing more than wounded pride;
> Remorse thro' horror into hell is driven,
> While true repentance always leads to heaven."

Nor is repentance to be confounded with "saying one's prayers"; or "doing penance"; or "making new resolutions"; or "breaking off some bad habit"; or "going to prayer meeting"; or "giving to charity." Repentance is a radical change of mind, thought, and purpose with reference to the great fundamentals; God, man, sin, righteousness and Christ: a change of mind accompanied by a change of feeling, and leading to a change of conduct and character; involving conviction, contrition and confession of sin; a turning away from sin, and acceptance of Christ. Thus it is intellectual, emotional and volitional; and involves a man's whole self.

> "Repentance is to leave
> The sins we loved before;
> And show that we in earnest grieve,
> By doing so no more."

In Dr. Stalker's "Trial and Crucifixion of Jesus Christ" there is a beautiful description given of "The Three Groups around the Cross." One group, sitting upon the ground near the foot of the cross, is made up of four Roman soldiers, the quaternion whose business it was to carry out the decrees of the court. They have done their work well. Having led Christ away to Golgotha, having laid and fastened the cross-piece upon the upright, they nail the Savior to the cross. Then they lift up the cross and its burden; and drop it into the hole which has been dug for it, making the cross fast with stakes and ropes. That work done, the soldiers sit down to divide the spoils; for they are his legal heirs, it being the custom that the garments of the condemned shall be the perquisites of the executioners. How little he had of material things! A turban, an outer garment, a girdle and a pair of sandals! Four articles for four soldiers. But there is a fifth article—the closely fitting, finely woven tunic. What shall they do with that? To rend it into four pieces would be to destroy its value. And so, in Roman fashion, they sit and cast lots to determine whose it shall be. What a picture of absolute indifference to the significant events of the hour! Yonder, within a few feet of them, is dying the Savior of the world; "a God upon a cross"; one who is tasting death even for the soldiers who crucify him; the supreme figure of all history. What a picture of those careless ones, who while away life's golden opportunities, playing at games of chance, and making light of the grandest themes of human or divine thought! What a picture of all those who are indifferent to Christ and righteousness! But a time will come when conscience will awake and memory will not be quieted. Then how mournful will be their souls' sad wail.

> "I thought of myself, I lived for myself,
> For myself and none beside;
> Just as if Jesus had never lived,
> As though He had never died."

Here is apathy indeed.

A second group about the cross, a much larger one, is composed of the members of the Sanhedrin; who, contrary to custom, are not content to have condemned the Nazarene, but have followed to the place of execution to gloat over the sufferings of the crucified. Along with the priests and scribes is a mixed crowd of people from Jerusalem, who are being stirred up by the leaders to hurl revilings at Christ. "Thou that destroyest the temple, and buildest it in three days, save thyself: if thou art the Son of God, come down from the Cross." "He saved others; himself he cannot save. He is the King of Israel; let him now come down from the cross, and we will believe on him." "He trusted on God; let him deliver him now, if he desireth him; for he said, I am the Son of

God." Thus did they there mock at Him, and scorn Him. What a picture that, of all those who are hostile to truth and Christ: whose desire is to tear down and destroy: who throw the weight of life and influence on the side of evil! Here is "not apathy but antipathy."

There was, however, another group about that cross that day. Like the first group, it was a small one; made up of some women, the three Marys; and John, the beloved disciple. Oh, how they love yonder man on the cross! The nails that pierce his hands have already pierced their hearts. They walked with him, talked with him, ministered to him; and now they are suffering with him, dying with him. Oh, how they love him! And yonder Christ on the cross, exhausted with hours of continuous agony, pained at the indifference of soldiers and the hate of scorners, must often have lifted his bloodshot eyes away from the indifferent and hostile, and lovingly looked upon these dear ones. How their presence must have soothed and rested his weary soul! How their love must have sustained his human spirit! Ah! here was "neither apathy, nor antipathy. Here was sympathy."

In one of these groups you will find yourself to-day. Jesus Christ divides the world. He is the touchstone of human character. What is your relationship to Him? Is it one of indifference, one of hostility, or one of loyal love? If you are honest with yourself, and with Him, you can and will realize your true condition.

It would be cruel to paint such a picture as this, were these groups already permanently fixed and unchangeable. But, blessed be God! they are in the forming. No great gulf is yet between. If you are not where you ought to be, and where you wish to remain, you can change your position. On that great day of crucifixion there was one man who did so. Since that day thousands have done so. The gospel of Matthew tells us, "And the robbers also that were crucified with him cast upon him the same reproach." That is, they both belonged to the second group, the group of scorners. But one of those thieves changed his position. I don't know whether he was in the judgment hall and heard Christ's answers to Pilate. I don't know whether he was on the porch, and saw the scourged and scorned Jesus; and heard Pilate, as he thrust the bleeding Christ before the throng, cry out, "Ecce Homo!" "Behold the Man!" I don't know whether he heard Christ speak to the weeping daughters of Jerusalem. But I feel sure that as the soldiers drove the nails through the palms and feet of the Savior, this thief heard Him pray for them, "Father, forgive them; they know not what they do." This thief must have noticed Jesus' look toward his widowed, desolate mother, and heard Him say, forgetful of Himself and thoughtful of her future, "Behold your son!" and to John, "Behold your mother!" What else he heard and saw, I know not. But as he thought, and listened, and looked at that Figure on the central cross, he "changed his mind"; his feelings became different; he changed his conduct. He left the company of the scornful; he joined the company of the sympathetic. He repented. And then he cried, "Jesus, remember me when thou comest into thy kingdom." "And Jesus said unto him, 'To-day shalt thou be with me in Paradise.'"

Two Kinds of Christians

1 Corinthians 3: 1-4.—"And I, brethren, could not speak unto you as unto spiritual, but as unto carnal, as unto babes in Christ. I fed you with milk, not with meat; for ye were not able to bear it; nay, not even now are ye able, for ye are yet carnal; for whereas there is among you jealousy and strife, are ye not carnal, and walk after the manner of men?"

Hebrews 5: 10-14.—"Named of God a high priest after the order of Melchizedek, of which we have many things to say, and hard of interpretation, seeing ye are become dull of hearing. For when by reason of the time ye ought to be teachers, ye have need again that some one teach you the rudiments of the first principles of the oracles of God, and are become such as have need of milk, and not of solid food. For every one that partaketh of milk is without experience of the word of righteousness; for he is a babe. But solid food is for full-grown men; even those who by reason of use have their senses exercised to discern good and evil."

BOTH Scripture and observation tell us that there are two kinds of Christians. One kind are carnal; one kind are spiritual; one babes; one full-grown: one children in Christian life and experience; one adults: one ruled by the world; the other ruled by the spirit.

There were not in New Testament days, nor in the New Testament churches, the two kinds of Christians in which some would have us believe; those who were "saints" in the sense of "sinlessly perfect ones," and those who were just ordinary, everyday Christians. Such a distinction exists neither in Scripture nor in fact; did not exist in the first century of the Christian Church; does not exist now. By the uniform usage of the New Testament all Christians are called "saints," "holy brethren," "partakers of a heavenly calling." The "saint," or "sanctified" person of the Old Testament, be he prophet, priest or king, was one who had been anointed with the sacred, flowing oil, and was set apart for sacred service. He was not a perfect person; he was not a sinless one. Even the High Priest, the most sanctified of all sanctified persons, must make an atonement first for his own sins, before he is fitted to make atonement for the sins of the people. The sanctified day was a day set apart for sacred use, and the sanctified place a place set apart for divine service. So all New Testament Christians are called "set-apart ones," "sanctified ones"; are "saved to serve," and called apart to live for God. "Ye are not your own. For ye were bought with a price: glorify God, therefore, in your body." "For the love of Christ constraineth us; because we thus judge, that one died for all, therefore all died; and he died for all, that they which live should no longer live unto themselves, but unto him who for their sakes died and rose again." All Christians are declared to be saints in Christ, and are destined to realized sainthood in proportion as they grow in grace, and in the knowledge of His will; and strive to attain to the fulness of the stature of manhood and womanhood through Christ. All in Christ are saints, but there are two kinds of saints. There were two kinds in the apostolic churches; there are two kinds in the churches now. The passages of Scripture in our study to-day clearly distinguish between two kinds of Christians; and suggest the characteristics of each.* There are carnal Christians, babes in Christ; and there are spiritual Christians, mature and well-developed. Nor is this distinction one of age in the Christian life. Some, who have only been Christians for a short time, manifest many evidences of maturity; while some, who by reason of time ought by now to be teachers, are still babes, needing milk and unable to digest solid food. Let us note four characteristics of the carnal Christian:

1. He is a babe. Now if one is only a few weeks or months old in the Christian life, we may expect such an one to be a babe, but we should not expect him to remain always a babe. A babe a

---

*For helpful suggestions here I am indebted to F. B. Meyer's "Way into the Holiest."

few weeks or months old is a delight indeed, but a babe fifteen or twenty years old is a monstrosity. If so in the physical world, why should it not be considered so in the spiritual world? Oh, you say, must we not become as little children before we can enter into the kingdom of God? And must we not retain the childlike spirit, if we are to make any true progress in spiritual life? Yes, most assuredly. There are features of the child-life that are always desirable; its faith, its teachableness, its simplicity, etc. But there are other features of the child-life, not to be cultivated; as its helplessness and lack of purpose. The babe is so helpless, weak and dependent. Its bones and muscles, its legs and back are not strong. And then, too, the babe does not live with any fixed purpose in view, nor direct its energies to any given goal. It drops one toy only to pick up another, it builds one castle in Spain, only to desert it, before it is half done, to plan another. So these carnal Christians are babes in helplessness, and in lack of lofty purpose. They have weak limbs and frail spines; they are not consumed with noble resolves, or driven on with a Christlike enthusiasm. They are babes.

2. They live upon milk. Now, milk is food partially digested by somebody else. The mother partially digests the food for the child, because the child has not the digestive and assimilative strength to do so for himself. So these carnal

Christians live upon milk, food partially digested by somebody else. They attach themselves to this or that preacher or teacher, and give as their basis of belief, "So and so says so." They are not able to give a good reason for the hope that is in them. They have no life in themselves. They do not search the Scriptures for themselves. They are like Jeremiah's broken cisterns that can hold no water. They are in no sense "a well of water springing up unto eternal life." Broken cisterns, empty and dry, they sit before the pastor on Lord's-day morning. He dumps into the cisterns a bucket full, a barrel full, a hogshead full of living water, howsoever much he may have on hand, and, poor man, before twenty-four hours have passed, with afternoon gaieties and evening larks, almost all of the living water has leaked away; and by midweek prayer-meeting the cisterns are entirely dry. Oh, that they would come personally to the Christ and drink of Him, that out of them might flow rivers of living water!

3. These carnal Christians are sectarian. "For when one saith, I am of Paul; and another, I am of Apollos; are ye not men? (i. e., as previous verse shows, carnal and walk after manner of men?)" Don't misunderstand me. I believe in denominational loyalty. The more mature a Christian becomes, the more thoroughly will he believe the peculiar phases of truth emphasized by his own denomination, provided they are

TWO KINDS OF CHRISTIANS 165

worthy of belief. He will be a better Presbyterian, a better Methodist, a better Baptist, etc. I am not waging war against denominations, but against the narrow, sectarian spirit. How may we know whether we are sectarian? Which stands first in your heart? Your church or Jesus Christ? Is the Christian life for you synonymous with membership in your church? Or does the Christian life mean to you, above and beyond all things else, living fellowship with a personal Redeemer and Friend? He who puts his church first is sectarian. So is it with these carnal Christians. The Christian life to such is largely a matter of times and places, of church and ceremony, of creed and ritual. It is largely external. Little is made of personal union with Christ, and of a Christ-like life through faith in and fellowship with Jesus. Much is made of form and external proprieties. Life is always large and free, the spirit means liberty. Sectarian form is often small and dwarfing. Every denomination can furnish examples similar to the following incident. I once heard of a man who, from the steps of a platform, was attempting to address a large audience. He was so small that the audience requested him to go up higher upon the steps that they might see him. He did so. Again the cry came from the audience, "Higher! higher! go up higher." And the little man replied, "I can't. I am as high as I can get. I'm a Baptist." High as you can get because you are a Baptist! May God have mercy upon your little shriveled-up soul. I'm a Baptist too, by conviction and by confession, as well as by birth and breeding. But is there nothing higher possible than to be a Baptist, or a Methodist; a Presbyterian, or a Disciple? Oh! to be a Christian is infinitely higher than to be any or all of these. Put loyalty to Christ first; then loyalty to the church.

4. Carnal Christians are unable "to discern good and evil." They have not grown in grace and in the knowledge of His will. They have not learned rightly to test things, and to approve only those things that are excellent. Their senses have not been "exercised by reason of use to discern good and evil." They are ever and anon doing things that are not worth while, that do not edify, or build up. They have no clear conception as to what is Christ-like, and what is not Christ-like. They are swayed by custom and circumstance rather than by conviction and character. These, then, are four characteristics of carnal Christians. They are babes; they live on milk; they are sectarian; they are unable to discern good and evil. In proportion as we approximate this condition, we approach the state of the carnal.

But how can we get away from the babyhood state and come into the mature life? Not by any short-cut method, nor by any "French taught in two weeks" plan. Nor shall we get it in any miraculous manner, as a direct and immediate answer to prayer. As well might the baby-boy pray, "O God! make me a full-grown, great, big man right off to-day." Such a prayer would not be in accord with God's will, nor in conformity with God's method of working. The baby-boy must fulfill certain well-known conditions, and in time he will become a "great, big man." He must eat, he must sleep, he must exercise and work, he must live in a healthy environment. So the baby Christian must fulfill certain well-known conditions, if he would become an adult Christian; and these conditions are similar to those of physical growth. He must accept the completed work of Christ, must step out on the promises, and live a life of implicit trust in Him. This is his rest. He must commune with God in prayer, learn of Him through the Scriptures, work for Him in his daily life. This is his food and exercise. He must also surround himself with helpful influences, and, through membership in the church and Christian societies, through attendance upon the house of God and mid-week prayer-meeting, through Christian friendship and fellowship, he must find that healthy environment which is necessary to the development of a strong Christian life. These plain conditions fulfilled by even the youngest and weakest of Christ's babes, will, with the factor of time added, most surely result in the longed-for Christian maturity.

And should you ask, "What are some of the striking features of the mature Christian life?" the answer is evident.

1. It is a life of personal possession. It is a life of conscious and constant communion with Christ. Creed and ritual, church and ceremony are precious, because they are a visible, external representation of that which is a personal, spiritual experience. The mature Christian feels a thrill in his soul as he cries out in the personal experience of David, "The Lord is my Shepherd." He loves to sing that blessed song of personal appropriation and conscious possession, "My Jesus, I love Thee, I know Thou art mine." That which is not personal is not powerful. Had S. F. Smith written "Our Country, 'Tis of Thee," we should never have adopted it as our national song. But when he had the genius to write "My Country, 'Tis of Thee," he struck a responsive chord in every patriot's heart. And when the writer of the sweet song wrote "My Jesus," he struck a harp-string in the mature Christian's life. This sense of personal possession and fact of conscious communion carry with them Christian assurance. The mature Christian has no doubt of his salvation. He doesn't say, "I hope I may be saved." "I trust I am a Christian." He knows it. "I know Thou art mine." "One thing I know, that, whereas I was blind, now I see." "I know him whom I have believed, and I am per-

suaded that he is able to guard that which I have committed unto him against that day."

2. It is a life of personal purity. The adult Christian, with his sense of personal possession and conscious communion, recognizes the absolute necessity of personal purity in his walk. He knows that only those are really blessed who are pure in heart. They alone see God. He regards himself as a son of God, a brother of Jesus Christ, a child of a Heavenly Father. "Like as he which called you is holy, be ye yourselves also holy in all manner of living; because it is written, 'Ye shall be holy; for I am holy.'" He reckons himself to be dead unto sin, but alive unto God. He knows he comes far short of actual personal righteousness, but the desire and design of his life are to "do always those things which please Him." He feels that he must be about his Father's business. Jesus has said to him, "You are the salt of the earth"; "You are the light of the world"; "You shall witness of these things." The mature Christian recognizes that the world does not see the invisible, though living, Christ; except as it sees Him in the Christian. Not "the gospel according to Matthew," nor "the gospel according to Mark"; not "the gospel according to Luke," nor "the gospel according to John"; but the fifth gospel, "the gospel according to you and me," is the gospel that the world reads. What sort of a gospel is "the gospel according to

you and according to me"? Is it an argument for Christ and Christianity? Or is it an argument against Christ? Does the sensitive soul incline more strongly to become a follower of Him, because that soul knows your life and mine? Or do we discourage people by our lives from starting in the Christian life? Are we His representatives? If so, do we re-present Christ in our lives? Or do we mis-represent Him? The importance of these things the mature Christian realizes, and he aims to make his life, through Christ's help, a life of personal purity.

3. It is a life of persistent purpose. One of the undesirable features of the baby-life is its indecision, its lack of definite purpose. The child is carried here and there by every freak of fancy, unstable in all his ways. He lives for the immediate present and the gratification of each passing whim. On the contrary a prominent feature of all healthy maturity is the presence of some strong motive power and noble purpose, which give direction to one's endeavors and act as a compass in life. This persistent purpose gives steadiness and poise to one's living; and lifts one above the dreary, dry drudgery of the commonplace. For the Christian there can be but one highest motive, "For me to live is Christ." To live for Him, to win fruit for Him, to become constantly more and more like Him. One resolve for the mature Christian must always take prece-

dence of all others. "That I may gain Christ, and be found in him, not having a righteousness of mine own, even that which is of the law, but that which is of God by faith: that I may know him and the power of his resurrection and the fellowship of his sufferings, being conformed unto his death; if by any means I may attain unto the resurrection of the dead." "One thing I do . . . I press on toward the goal, unto the prize of the high calling of God in Christ Jesus. Let us therefore, as many as be perfect (mature), be thus minded."

4. It is a life of perpetual progress. At first one might make the mistake of supposing that maturity of life means a cessation of growth. But it is not thus in the normal life. There will be a constant deepening and sweetening and broadening of the soul's experience. The path of the righteous will grow brighter and brighter unto the perfect day. The more one develops into maturity of life, the more one realizes his own short-comings, and the loftiness of the heights of holiness. No really mature person ever thinks that he has already attained the goal. The more one really knows, the less he thinks he knows; and the more he sees there is to learn. So it is in all departments of life. So it is in the Christian's experience. Paul, in the maturity of a rich Christian life, said, in deepest humility and without any consciousness of spiritual superi-

ority, "Not that I have already obtained, or am already made perfect: but I press on, if so be that I may apprehend that for which also I was apprehended by Christ Jesus. Brethren, I count not myself yet to have apprehended, but one thing I do, forgetting the things which are behind (the failures of the past, the attainments of the past), and stretching forward to the things which are before, I press on toward the goal . . . Let us therefore, as many as be perfect, be thus minded."

5. It is a life of permanent power. One great reason why our churches do not have more power with God and man is because there is in them such a large body of carnal Christians; Christians who are babes in Christ; in whom the world rules; who upon the foundation, Christ, are building hay, wood and stubble; who, by the grace of God, shall be saved, yet so as by fire; whose works shall be burned and destroyed, and they themselves shall suffer loss; whose lives count for little or nothing so far as permanent power is concerned. The primary need of Christ, of the church, of the world to-day, is not for more professing Christians, but for a better type and grade of Christians; not for more disciples, but for more in the disciples; nor for more branches on the vine, but for more on each branch; not for more foliage, but for more fruit. But we must not pray directly for more fruit, but first for more

love and more life. God will not hang rich, red, ripe, luscious fruit upon rotten boughs; or grow good grapes upon impoverished vines. If it is fruit that is desired, let us then remember that "fruits come from roots." Only maturity of life means much fruit. For the mature life can no more fail of fruit, and be lacking in permanent power, than the sun can cease to shine.

Let us then flee away from babyhood with its weakness and feeding upon milk, with its sectarianism and lack of discernment Let us, by using the means of grace, grow in grace and in the knowledge of His will, and strive to attain to the fulness of the stature of manhood and womanhood in Christ. Then we shall come into a life of personal possession, personal purity, persistent purpose, perpetual progress and permanent power. Then will life be, indeed, an inspiration and a joy; and at its earthly close we may say with grand old Paul:

"I have fought the good fight,
I have finished the course,
I have kept the faith;
Henceforth there is laid up for me the crown of righteousness."

"Life's race well run;
Life's work well done;
Life's crown well won."

Individual Responsibility for Souls

Ezekiel 33:7.—"*So thou, son of man, I have set thee a awatchman unto the house of Israel; therefore hear the word at my mouth, and give them warning from me.*"
Matt. 5:13.—"*Ye are the salt of the earth.*"
Matt. 5:14.—"*Ye are the light of the world.*"
Acts 1:8.—"*And ye shall be my witnesses.*"
Revelation 22:17.—"*And he that heareth, let him say 'Come.'*"

IN the fourteenth chapter of Romans and in the seventh verse we find these significant words, "For none of us liveth unto himself and none dieth unto himself." This striking sentence was written by Paul over eighteen hundred years ago. If it meant anything then, what must it mean now? Eighteen hundred years ago the world seemed large. Men lived far apart from one another, in isolated communities, mutually ignorant and mutually suspicious of each other. But to-day isolation is no longer possible. The world has become small. Modern science has made the whole round world one small neighborhood. As Dr. Josiah Strong has put it: "Steam and electricity have mightily compressed the earth: the elbows of the nations touch." If, in that far-off time of isolation and separation, Paul could write, "None of us liveth unto himself and no one dieth unto himself," what added weight of truth is found in his words to-day! The intricate intimacies of modern life are remarkable for their closeness. We have all been shoved together into nearness of relationship; and these relationships bring responsibility. No longer is it possible for individual or nation to live alone, apart from relationship and without responsibility. We are born into relationships, we live in the midst of them, we die in the midst of them. We are related to God, to self, to each other; and our relationships determine for us our duties. The effect of relationship and influence may be illustrated from the physical world. In the world of matter the molecules of matter all touch one upon another. No molecule exists apart from its fellows. And so when I move my hand through space, I disturb all the molecules of air which are within my immediate reach, which molecules disturb other molecules, until the wave of disturbance goes round the world. Drop a pebble upon the surface of a lake, and from that small point of disturbance a series of concentric circles will be formed, larger and larger, larger and larger, until they cover the surface of the whole water. So in the world of persons, we are related one to another. No one stands absolutely alone. No one lives who is entirely without influence. Every one is helping or hindering others every day of his life. There is no flower that blooms even on the dizziest mountain peak or in the deepest dell, but that the air is sweeter because of it. There is no cesspool anywhere, however hidden, but that the air is fouler because of it. Nor has any one of us to-day had a thought or desire heavenward, but that the world is better for it. Nor has any one of us had a thought or desire of evil to-day, but that this world of ours has swung a little nearer the pit. But it is not of general relationships, nor of responsibilities in general that I wish now to speak; but of a certain specific relationship, and of a particular responsibility. We enjoy listening to general truths. We do not like specific applications. David was entertained by Nathan's beautiful parable of the Ewe Lamb. He was only convicted of sin, when Nathan made the general specific, and said, "Thou art the man." Let none of us, then, try to hide behind a general truth, but let us be individually honest with a personal duty. God's first question to man in the Garden was, "Where art thou?" This question, I presume, the majority of my audience have already answered. But there was a second question which soon followed, "Where is thy brother?" How are you answering this question? In the spirit of Cain, are you trying to cast off all responsibility by saying, "Am I my brother's keeper?" Or in the spirit of the second Adam, the Christ of Nazareth, are you going out to seek and to save the lost? Whom are you following, Cain or Christ? "Where is thy brother?" This, then, is the theme for our present consideration, individual responsibility for the salvation of souls.

1. There are not two moral standards laid down in Scripture; one for the preacher or evangelist, and another for the ordinary Christian. The preacher or evangelist is only the ordinary Christian doing, with all of his time and energy, that which every Christian is bound by duty and love to do. All of us have been saved to serve. All of us are sons of God, and are called to work in our Father's vineyard. All are commissioned and sent forth to do the Father's business. There is not a verse or passage in all Scripture, from Genesis to Revelation, properly translated and interpreted in the light of its context, and in full view of the gradualness and progressiveness of revelation; not a single verse or passage which teaches, or even intimates, that the preacher, evangelist or trained worker ought to feel the burden for souls, while the ordinary Christian and layman ought not to feel it. These two moral standards are not Scriptural. All Scripture in its trend and in its teaching is opposed to such

a double standard of duty. One marked difference between the Old Covenant and the New Covenant, as foretold in Old Testament prophecy and fulfilled in New Testament days (as the eighth chapter of Hebrews makes clear), lies just in this fact that in the days of the Old Covenant God's Spirit was poured out only upon a few persons in a generation, upon prophet, priest or king; while in the days of the New Covenant the Spirit is poured out upon all the members of the kingdom. Recall for a moment that wonderful prophecy of Joel. A severe locust plague had been followed by a drought. The people in their distress turned to God with fasting and prayer. In answer to prayer God removed the locusts, and, through the pouring out of rain, the drought. And then God gave a wonderful promise. "And it shall come to pass afterward (using that indefinite phrasing of which the prophets were fond) that I will pour out my spirit upon all flesh; and your sons and your daughters shall prophesy, your old men shall dream dreams, your young men shall see visions: and also upon the servants and upon the handmaids in those days will I pour out my spirit." Eight hundred years and more rolled around. Jesus lived, died, rose again, ascended to the Father and sent his Spirit upon the company of disciples at Pentecost—and that Spirit rested upon each one of them. Those who witnessed the wonders of that day said, "These men are filled with new wine." But Peter, standing up with the eleven said, "These are not drunken, as ye suppose; seeing it is but the third hour of the day; but this is that which hath been spoken by the prophet Joel, 'And it shall be in the last days, saith God, I will pour forth of my Spirit upon all flesh: and your sons and your daughters shall prophesy, and your young men shall see visions, and your old men shall dream dreams: Yea, and on my servants and on my hand-maidens in those days will I pour forth of my Spirit and they shall prophesy.'" To prophesy does cot mean to foretell so much as to forth tell. A prophet was one who spoke for another. God said to Moses, "And Aaron, thy brother, shall be thy prophet," (thy spokesman). Now Joel foretold that, while then only a few, prophet, priest or king, had the gift of God's spirit and were commissioned to speak for Him, the time would come when things would be different. The time would come when, as God had abundantly poured out the rain, He would abundantly pour out His Spirit; not simply upon an official prophet, priest or king, but upon all, irrespective of age, sex or condition: young and old, bond and free, male and female, all should have the gift of God's Spirit, and he privileged, yes, commissioned to declare God's truth. This was fulfilled and is being fulfilled in this New Testament time, the age of the Spirit. So we find Christians everywhere addressed thus: "Ye are the light of the world;" "Ye are the salt of the earth;" "And ye shall be my witnesses;" "The Spirit and the Bride say, 'Come,' and him that heareth, let him say, 'Come'." This is the very genius of the New Testament plan of the world's salvation, that every one, who hears and heeds the message of salvation, is to go out and declare it unto his fellows. We are stewards of the manifold grace of God, and it is required of stewards that a man be found faithful. Christ's great commission to the Christian church recognizes no double standard of duty, but commands every disciple. "All power is given unto me, . . . go ye therefore, . . . make disciples, . . . and lo: I am with you all the days."

2. Again, let us note the danger of our times. In the business world to-day we do much of our business through middlemen, or commissioners. For example, I was recently in Greenville, Mich., an important potato market of that State. Now the farmers who live about Greenville, and who raise large quantities of excellent potatoes, do not sell these potatoes directly to the consumers, but bring them into North Greenville and sell them to the potato commissioners, allowing the middlemen a profit, or margin, for the selling of the potatoes. The commissioners sell them to the wholesalers, the wholesalers to retailers, the retailers to the consumers, and each gets a

profit, or margin, on the sales. In other words the middlemen are paid a living by the farmers for selling their potatoes for them. Thus much of the business of to-day is done. Now the danger of the times is just this: that people shall begin to try to meet their religious obligations too much in this same spirit. You say, "Why do we pay our pastor a salary? Why do we support the church? Why do we engage an evangelist, unless it is that they may do our religion for us, and save those whom we ought to be saving?" There is, to be sure, some truth implied in your query. But we must ever keep in mind that these personal, religious obligations cannot be easily nor safely shifted from layman to preacher. These responsibilities are ours, individually, and whenever we try to hire others to meet them for us, we ourselves suffer great personal loss, and the kingdom is hindered. Some years ago in many of our young cities there was a volunteer fire brigade. In every home was a bucket in the hall, full of water, marked "For fire," ready for use. When the village, or city, fire bell rang, everybody dropped everything and ran for the bucket, and the fire. And, through hearty co-operation and a multitude of helpers, the conflagration was soon extinguished. But to-day, when the fire bell rings, we listen to the number, look at our fire card, and, if the fire is not in the neighborhood of our store or home, we leisurely pursue our pleasure. We have hired somebody to fight our fires for us. In old New England days it was the custom that services should be begun in the meeting-houses "at early candle-lighting." As the people came to church, each brought a candle, and something with which to light it; when enough lighted candles had come to light the meeting-house, services would begin. But to-day, we have our oil-lights, or gas-lights, or our electric-lights in our churches; the janitor is hired to light them; and we leave our candles and our lights at home. And, believe me, there are places where, if you should wait until enough lighted candles had arrived to light up the meeting-house, before you should begin the service, services would never begin. We hire somebody to light up the church for us, and we leave our candles at home. Even as Mr. Moody was told in Scotland, when he complained of there being no fire in a certain church in extremely cold weather, "No, we have no fire: we expect you to warm us up," so do people here sometimes expect the preacher or pastor or evangelist to do all of the work, carry all of the burdens, and save all of the souls.

3. Yet the commands of God are individual; relationships are individual; responsibility is individual. The Bible everywhere treats men and women as individuals. We are not all alike, not blocks, not cogs in a wheel, not things; but per-

RESPONSIBILITY FOR SOULS

sons. No book in the world has done so much for the individual man, has so emphasized his worth and his personality, as has the Bible. It has brought about the abolition of slavery; it has introduced popular education; it has led to the building of hospitals; it has lessened the atrocities of war as well as the possibility of war; it has led to many labor-reforms, etc., largely through its emphasis of the fact and the worth of the individual. Both nature and revelation emphasize the fact of individuality. We are born as individuals; we live as individuals; we die as individuals. We are saved as individuals; Christ loves us and died for us as individuals, "tasting death for every man"; we are lost as individuals; we shall be judged as individuals. "For we must all be made manifest before the judgment-seat of Christ; that each one may receive the things done in the body, according to what he hath done, whether it be good or bad." God's commands are individual. "Thou shalt love the Lord thy God with all thy heart," and "Thou shalt love thy neighbor as thyself," are the two great commands of the Savior; and both of them are individual and personal. Our ability is the measure of our responsibility. God expects us to do only what we can do. If there is a single soul anywhere whom we can influence to come to Christ, if we do not so do, God can rightly hold us responsible for the consequences of our negligence. If a single soul through our faithlessness is lost, who would have been saved had we been faithful, then, in some real sense, God can and will hold us responsible for that soul. This seems to be the plain teaching of Ezekiel 33 as well as the plain implication of other passages of Scripture. How earnest and active ought each one of us to be! There is a question in the minds of some people as to what is the present position and work of the church of Christ. Is the church a fine palace, filled with beauty and luxury, in the midst of a cool grove, with music and gaiety resounding through its halls and its rooms filled with pleasure seekers? Or is it a lighthouse out upon the reefs, its rays of brightness and light shining far out over the deep? Which is it, a palace full of pleasure seekers, or a lighthouse, filled with life-savers? But a more personal question is, "How does your life and mine count?" Are we helping to make our church simply a pleasure palace, or are we helping to make it a life-saving station? How does your life count in your church? Some people are wondering whether the church is a brass-trimmed yacht out on a pleasant cruise; or whether it is a life-boat, thrust out through the surf, each man pulling an oar. Which is it, life-boat or pleasure yacht? How does your life count in your church? Is your church more of a life-boat, because you are a member there; or is your church more of a pleasure yacht, because of your membership in it? Which way does *your* life count? Do you recall the story of Old Skipper Ireson? Ireson was a fisherman in Marblehead. With his mates, he had been out at the Banks, and had made a large haul of fish. On their way home they sighted a vessel near by, flying a flag of distress. We don't know who was really to blame, whether it was Ireson or his men. At any rate, somebody said, "Oh, don't pay any attention to that flag. We're fishermen. We don't belong to any life-saving station. Our business is to catch fish, not to save men; and we're very successful at our business too." And so they made haste to port in order to forestall the market, and sell their fish at a good price. They did so, I suppose. But, you know, that night the widows and women of Marblehead "took old Floyd Ireson for his hard heart, and tarred and feathered him and carried him in a cart." Why was it? What had he done? Ah, that was just it. He hadn't done anything. He had simply made the mistake of saying, as some of you are saying, "My business is something else. I'm not a life-saver."

4. There are times of peculiar privilege and peculiar peril, which times are also times of peculiar and special responsibility. Any church which determines to go into a special effort to save the lost, which opens up its doors night after night and day after day for evangelistic services,

takes upon itself a terrible responsibility. I don't know whether you appreciated what you were doing when you decided to undertake these meetings. You have, I trust, opened out before yourselves a door of great privilege. I know that you have brought upon yourselves peculiar peril and a time of special responsibility. At such a time as this many souls are very sensitive. It is a time when it is easy to lead people to Christ. It is also a time when it is very easy to offend and harden and turn people away from Christ. Oh, how carefully and prayerfully we ought to walk at such a time as this! How wise we need to be to see and to seize every possible chance to take advantage of the tide and bring people into the harbor of life! Well might a great preacher say, "I always pray for such times, but I also dread them." It is a time of such peril. The rain that falls softens some soil, and hardens other soil. When the seed is sown, some will fall by the wayside, some on stony ground, some among thorns, some into good ground. "What shall the harvest be?" People will come to these meetings conscious of the purpose of the meetings; people will come to these meetings with the call of God inviting their souls to submission; people will come to these meetings expecting a plain personal appeal from the pulpit; people will come to these meetings rightly expecting a warm, cordial reception in the pew; people will come to

RESPONSIBILITY FOR SOULS 187

these meetings and go out from these meetings never again to be as they have been; some will be better, some worse, some more inclined toward faith, some more hardened against all religion, some with souls forever saved, some never again to attend any special meetings, only to go on and on in indifference and sin. What shall the results of these meetings be? What are you and I willing to make them? Down in an Ohio city a few years ago I was holding a special series of meetings in the Baptist church, and was told that the large high-school building, which adjoined the church, stood upon the water-shed of Ohio. The water which fell upon one side of the roof ran into the headwaters of the Sandusky River, down the Sandusky into Lake Erie and into Lake Ontario, and down the St. Lawrence into the North Atlantic Ocean. The water which fell on the other side of the roof went into the headwaters of the Scioto River, down the Scioto into the Ohio, down the Ohio into the Mississippi, down the Mississippi into the Gulf of Mexico. Now, for purposes of illustration, it is not at all difficult to imagine a drop of water about to fall right above the ridge-pole of that roof. The slightest breeze, either from the north or from the south, will change the entire future history of that drop of water. The ridge-pole and the moment of falling constitute a crisis in the little life of that rain-drop. If the breeze is a warm southern breeze, the drop will fall upon the north side of the roof and start on its long journey to the North Atlantic Ocean. If the breeze is a cold northern one, the drop of rain will fall upon the southern side of the roof, and start on a long journey away down to the Gulf of Mexico. So there will come ridges of destiny, crises into human lives, in these meetings. The business of an evangelist is to bring these crises. The purpose of these meetings is to bring people to decision. What shall your influence be? By a cold northern blast, by an unsympathetic handshake, by half-hearted singing, by lack of prayerfulness in demeanor, and in heart life, by general indifference to the spiritual purposes of the occasion, will you discourage a sensitive soul, destroy a heavenly impulse, drive away God's Holy Spirit, and hinder some person from accepting Christ? Or, by a sweet prayerful spirit, by a warm genial personality, by a hearty welcome and decent hand-shake, by soulful singing and attentive presence, will you cheer and encourage, as with a warm, sunny southern breeze, some sensitive soul to start on a blessed journey of life, upward and heavenward and Christ-ward, until at last there shall be no sin which has not been conquered, and no excellence which has not been acquired? What part will you choose to have in these meetings?

God is going to bless us. There is no doubt of

RESPONSIBILITY FOR SOULS 189

that. He has promised always to bless His truth, and I believe that in a special way His Spirit broods over such a meeting as this. But, whether the blessing which we shall surely receive, shall be a large one, or a small one, will depend very largely upon us. We can limit it, or we can enlarge it. We can hinder it or we can help it. Would you know how specially to help? Four things may here and now be mentioned. (1) Nothing but united, earnest effort can bring the largest blessing. We must be willing for the time to side-track all extras, dress-making, parties, special entertainments, etc., and give the meetings the first place. (2) We ought to have a prayer-time and a prayer-list. Once every day, in closet, in the home, in the store, on the street, or wherever we may happen to be, we ought to lift our hearts in earnest prayer that God may specially bless these meetings, bless the pastor and evangelist, bless the church-members and those in the Sunday Schools, bless the unsaved; and, above all, let each one pray for himself, "O God, help me to be helpful." "Search me, O God, and know my heart; try me and know my thoughts; and see if there be any way of wickedness in me and lead me in the way everlasting." Not only a prayer-time but a prayer-list. We must not only talk to men about God. We need also to talk to God about men, and we should do this first. Don't have the prayer-list too long. We need to concentrate as well as consecrate. "To keep shot from scattering put in only one shot." We need definiteness of aim. The man who says, "I'm praying that the whole town may be converted," is probably not praying or working very definitely for anybody. Start your prayer-list right now, if you have not already done so. Somebody in your home, in your neighborhood, in your Sunday-School class, in your social sphere, ought to be saved in these meetings. You know who it is. Begin now to pray for that one; then follow up your definite prayers with definite work, and God will greatly bless. (3) Make one call each day in the interest of the meetings. I don't mean a formal call, nor what once was named "a religious call." What is desired is that you should summon up all of the graciousness of your personality, and in the most interested and persuasive way possible, speak to at least one person each day about the meetings. If you can't say something good about the meetings, don't say anything. Make up your mind to be, if possible, a walking advertisement among your friends in the interest of these services. (4) Make an earnest and honest attempt to bring one person with you to each service. Make an engagement with a friend. Call at the house for him. It will help you to be unselfish, will put you, through self-sacrifice, into a better spirit for the meetings, and you'll share with your friend a blessing. These four suggestions will be of great assistance to the meetings, if followed faithfully by you. Is it too much to ask you for ten days honestly to try to do these four things; put the meetings first, have a prayer-time and a prayer-list, make one call or speak to some one each day persuasively about the meetings, make an honest attempt to bring somebody with you to each service? Perhaps it is too much to ask for the pastor's sake, for the church's sake, for your own sake, for the community's sake, for some soul's sake. Is it too much to ask for Christ's sake? For His sake, will you try?

Paul's Prayer for the Philippians

Philippians 1:9-11.—"*And this I pray, that your love may abound yet more and more in knowledge and all discernment, so that ye may approve the things that are excellent, that ye may be sincere and void of offense unto the day of Christ; being filled with the fruits of righteousness, which are through Jesus Christ, unto the glory and praise of God.*"

THE apostle Paul was not only a man of intense activity, but he was also a man of much prayer. That he was much given to prayer appears not only from the frequent mention of the fact in Luke's historical material in the book of Acts, and from the frequent mention of it by Paul himself in practically all of his epistles; but it appears also from the fact that he knew how to pray Prayer is a fine art. It is something that must be learned. The disciples said to Jesus, "Lord, teach us to pray, even as John taught his disciples to pray." Paul had learned through much toil, through large and varied experiences, through patient practice, through hours of devout meditation upon the Scriptures, how to pray. He was a master in prayer.

A splendid way for us to learn how to pray, a splendid way to learn how to deepen and to enrich our prayers, to learn how to keep them out of ruts and vain repetitions (and there is a considerable amount of inanity and empty phrasing in much prayer), is to make a study of the prayers of the Bible. The psalms are full of prayers, very appropriate to the lives of men and women of to-day. Let us collect some of them, meditate upon them, learn them, get into the true spirit of them, and make them our own. The historical books of the Old Testament have in them some very fine prayers. By studying prayers, we may teach ourselves how to pray. The gospels and the Acts have in them some very helpful prayers. Let us prayerfully drink in their spirit, and we ourselves shall know the better how to pray. In Paul's epistles we have much material upon this very important subject. In the first chapter of Colossians is a fine example of prayer, also in the first chapter of Paul's love-letter to the Philippians. Either of these passages is worthy of special study. We can take only the one from Philippians at this time for the subject of our meditation. The Philippians were very dear to Paul, and Paul was very dear to them. He doubtless felt that they were nearer his ideal of a church than any company of believers that he had been privileged to gather. There was among them very little of irregularity in doctrine and practice. They were closely in sympathy with his work and with spiritual things. Paul could open his very heart to them, and we find in this letter more of the inner motives of the great apostle to the Gentiles expressed than in any other of his epistles. Paul had already received many tokens of the love of these Philippians. Twice before the occasion of this letter of gratitude, they had sent to relieve his necessities. And now that Paul is a prisoner at Rome, chained to a Roman soldier and no longer able to make his own living, the Philippians send to him by Epaphroditus an expression of love and that which would supply his need. In the spring of the year, as Epaphroditus is about to return to Philippi, Paul sends by his hand to the Philippians this letter of affection and grateful appreciation. After the usual salutation, the apostle expresses his thanksgiving for their past life, his confidence in their future, and his earnest prayer for their present. "And this I pray, that your love may abound yet more and more in knowledge and all discernment; so that ye may approve the things that are excellent; that ye may be sincere and void of offence unto the day of Christ; being filled with the fruits of righteousness, which are through Jesus Christ, unto the glory and praise of God." Surely such a prayer, at such a time, for such dear friends, and by such a master in prayer, is well worth earnest study. Paul does not pray for these Philippians that their knowledge may abound, nor yet that their influence may abound, nor yet that their physical health may abound, nor that their friends may abound, nor that their wealth may abound. He prays for that which is their fundamental need, that their love may abound. He who said, "Faith, hope, love, but the greatest of these is love," recognizes that the real need of life is more love; love for Christ, love for each other, love for those for whom the Savior died. He prays not for a love which may fill one little corner of the heart and life, he prays not for a love which may fill half of the heart; but for a love which abounds, and for a love which keeps on growing and abounding more and yet more. But this love for which he prays must not be empty emotion, or zeal without knowledge, but love founded on and increasing with increasing knowledge. Love without knowledge is apt to be weak and without endurance. Knowledge without love may be as cold and lifeless as marble. But love which increases as knowledge increases, and knowledge which increases as love is deeper and broader, when linked together, constitute the very dynamite of God. But there is a peculiar kind of knowledge which Paul would have them possess, that knowledge which leads to discrimination. One of the great problems of life is to know what is worth while; what is of real value and what is comparatively worthless. In proportion as we discriminate between values and approve only those things which are excellent, we are in the path of real progress. If we are really and truly growing in grace and in the knowledge of His will, the road over which we have thus far journeyed will be strewn with cast-off things, things to which we once clung and which we thought were valuable, but which we have since learned were "weights." We shall be coming more and more to "cast aside the weights and the sins that so easily beset us, and to run with patience the race set before us." Now Paul prays for these friends that their love may abound more and yet more in knowledge and all discernment, that they may test things and approve only those things that are excellent. And what would be the logical result of a life of love, abounding more and yet more in knowledge and all discernment, testing things and approving only what is excellent? It would be a life "sincere and void of offence unto the day of Christ." A sincere life is a life which can bear the searching light of the noontide sun, a life in which there is no pretence, no sham, no make-believe, a life which is as it appears to be; while a life "void of offence unto the day of Christ" is a life in which there is nothing over which the possessor would stumble, and nothing which would cause others to stumble;

a life which will be able to stand the test of that day when all secrets shall be told, and the hidden shall be revealed. Such a life of love, abounding with knowledge, leading to the testing of things and the approval only of excellent things, resulting in sincerity and absence of any cause of stumbling, even to the day of Christ, will be "filled with the fruits of righteousness, which are through Jesus Christ, unto the glory and praise of God." Not a little fruit here and there, but "filled with fruits"; fruits which are the result of right living and result in righteous character; fruits which do not come through one's own unaided efforts, but "through Jesus Christ"; fruits which result not in self-glorification, but "unto the glory and praise of God." Such is the wonderful course of thought in Paul's prayer for the Philippians. He begins with abounding love, he ends with abounding fruitfulness. Every link in the golden chain is necessary, and necessary in the order named. Omit a single link, and the beauty and strength of the chain are gone. Abounding love coupled with abounding knowledge, the testing of things and approval of that only which is excellent, a life sincere and void of offence unto the day of Christ, a life filled with fruits, through Christ, unto the glory and praise of God. How logical it all is! There can never be abounding fruit apart from the fulfilling of these necessary conditions. We often long and pray for more fruit. Let us remember that "fruits come from roots" and see to it that we fulfill the plain conditions of a harvest.

Prof. Drummond once said that if any Christian would take that remarkable chapter on love, first Corinthians, thirteen, and read it once a day carefully and prayerfully for two years, it would marvelously enrich and deepen his Christian experience. I feel similarly about this prayer of Paul. If you will study it and learn it (it is very easy to commit, as it is so logical) and incorporate it into your daily petitions for two years, it will wonderfully enlarge your conception of the Christian life, will enrich your prayers, and deepen your spiritual experience. Will you try it for yourself?

Thankfulness[*]

Ephesians 5:18-20.—"*And be not drunken with wine, wherein is riot, but be filled with the spirit; speaking one to another in psalms and hymns and spiritual songs, singing and making melody with your heart to the Lord; giving thanks always for all things in the name of our Lord Jesus Christ to God, even the Father.*"

IF we were to study the subject of prayer, as it is illustrated by the prayers of the Bible, we should be impressed with the thought that there must be, either expressed or implied, five elements in all true prayer; and that these elements too will occur in the same general order. There will be first an ascription of praise and thanksgiving to God. This is most fitting on the part of a helpless creature coming into the pres-

---

[*] Ever since I gave my life to Christ I have been trying to emphasize by life and song and sermon the duty and the privilege of thankfulness. During the last seven years, while life has been lived in a wheel-chair, I have considered it to be an especial privilege and duty to speak upon this pleasant theme. Surely the Father grants to those of us, whose lives are in the world's view so broken and saddened, a dark background upon which we can the more easily present the thought of Christian cheerfulness.

ence of a benevolent Creator; or of a dependent son addressing a provident Heavenly Father. Then there will follow an humble confession of sin. This surely will rush to the lips of him who has any conception at all of the heinousness of sin, of his own faults and failings, and of the holiness of God. Then, thirdly, there will be a pleading of God's promises, which promises are the basis of approach unto God, and an encouragement to faith. Then there will follow a recalling of past mercies and blessings received, which still further will stimulate faith. And lastly there will be definite and persistent petition. A fine example of such prayer, where these five elements are clearly manifest, is found in the first chapter of the wonderful book of Nehemiah, Nehemiah's prayer when his heart was burdened for Jerusalem.

One very important element in true prayer we are apt to overlook, or to slight, the element of praise and thankfulness. We have almost forgotten how to cry "Hallelujah!" "Praise ye the Lord!" And yet the spirit of true prayer and of true praise go ever hand in hand. It matters little whether you call the world's great song book "The Prayers of David" or "The Psalms of David"; for praise and prayer are sisters. Therefore Paul writes to the Colossians, "Continue steadfastly in prayer, watching therein with thanksgiving"; and to the Philippians, "With thanksgiving, let your requests be made known unto God." We do not so often fail in our asking as in our thanking. We are in danger of becoming a family of beggars. Our prayers and our lives are in danger of being sadly marred and scarred by a lack of gratitude. Our prayers and our lives are in danger of losing much of their sweetness and their power through a minimum of praise; life thus becomes warped and selfish, displeasing to God and powerless with men. We have an annual Thanksgiving Day in our national calendar. Nationally and personally it may be a curse to us, or a blessing. If we take advantage of the custom to live a life of fussing and complaining for three hundred and sixty-four days of the year, or three hundred and sixty-five days if it happens to be leap-year; and then soothe to sleep an already drowsy conscience by tacking on an appendix of gratitude to our Thanksgiving Day prayer, only to spend the rest of the day in gormandizing or dissipation, the day will be a hindrance to us rather than a help. But if the presence of such a day in our personal or national calendar will cause us to stop and think of our many blessings and our ill-desert, and will help us to cultivate the spirit of gratitude and to live more thankful lives, then the day will always be to us a personal as well as a national blessing.

Not only is thankfulness an important element in all true prayer, but it is also to be noted that men and women who are pre-eminent for real piety are pre-eminent for praise. A few examples from biblical history will make this abundantly evident. Moses was a man of true piety. He was pre-eminent in praise. All through his long and useful life he kept setting up memorials of God's mercies, and emphasized the importance of the festivals of thanksgiving. The whole book of Deuteronomy is largely made up of Moses' great thanksgiving addresses, given at the close of his life, when he lovingly recounted and called upon the people to "remember all the way that the Lord" their God had led them. David, the man after God's own heart, was pre-eminent for praise. Of all Old Testament characters he seems most near to the majority of us, because of the wide diversity of his experiences. David had such a checkered career; touched life at so many points; seemed so human. Like his greater Son, he was tempted and tried in all points like as we are, and so in some experience of his life he resembles every other life. And yet, during all of the varied experiences of his varied life, we find him to be a man of song and praise. No matter when his psalms may have been written; in the seclusion and quiet of his shepherd hours; or when he was the favorite at the court of the king; or when he was fleeing as a refugee from the wrath of Saul; or when he was at the height of his power as king over all

Israel; or when his own sin and family troubles were bringing him in sorrow to his grave; in every hour of his life he finds some occasion for gratitude, and sings in almost every psalm, "Praise ye the Lord." Yes, in spite of all his failings, in many ways David was the man after God's own heart; penitent for his sin, aspiring toward the best, thankful at all times. Daniel, too, pre-eminent for piety, was pre-eminent for praise. Even when an exile and captive in victorious Babylon, three times a day even at the risk of his life, he opened his windows toward Jerusalem, and upon his knees "prayed and gave thanks before his God as he did aforetime" (i. e., as was his custom).

When we turn to New Testament times we find in the lives of Jesus, and of his faithful pupil, Paul, remarkable illustration of the same truth, that true piety and praise go hand in hand. All through the life of Jesus, a life of sorrow, loneliness and hardest toil and trial, there runs a glad theme of thanksgiving and praise; so that even under the shadow of the cross he cries out exultantly, "I thank Thee, O Father." In the life of Paul also we have a splendid illustration of the habit of thankfulness in all of the varied circumstances of life. For Paul, like David, had a very checkered career. Joy and sorrow, health and sickness, prosperity and adversity, the love of friends and the hatred of foes, all were a part of his lot. As he himself wrote to the Philippians, "I know how both to be abased and to abound, . . . both to be full and to be hungry." Paul tasted almost every experience possible in the whole gamut of human trial. Listen to his own list as given in 2 Cor. 11:23-28: "Are they ministers of Christ? (I speak as one beside himself.) I more; in labours more abundantly, in prisons more abundantly, in stripes above measure, in deaths oft. Of the Jews five times received I forty stripes save one. Thrice was I beaten with rods, once was I stoned, thrice I suffered shipwreck, a night and a day have I been in the deep; in journeyings often, in perils of rivers, in perils of robbers, in perils from my countrymen, in perils from the Gentiles, in perils in the city, in perils in the wilderness, in perils in the sea, in perils among false brethren; in labour and travail, in watchings often, in hunger and thirst, in fastings often, in cold and nakedness. Besides those things that are without, there is that which presseth upon me daily, anxiety for all the churches." And yet everywhere we find a ringing note of praise in all of Paul's life. His letters, written, some on the second missionary tour, some on the third missionary tour, some in the time of the first Roman imprisonment and some between two imprisonments or during a second imprisonment about to end in execution—his letters usually begin with thanksgiving and end with praise. Indeed the customary Pauline introduction is a salutation and then a paragraph of gratitude. "I thank my God always." If some people should talk to us about the duty of thankfulness, we should be tempted to say to them, "It's very easy for you to think and speak thus; for you have never had any very hard trials; life for you has always been rather smooth and pleasant." But when Paul, a man of so many troubles and such varied experiences, speaks of the duty and privilege of gratitude, we ought surely to give heed to him. Do you recall one of his experiences on his second missionary tour? It was at Philippi. Paul had scarcely recovered from his illness in Galatia. A divine call was heard from Macedonia, to which Paul, with Silas and other companions, had gladly responded. As they went to and fro in this important European town, they were often harassed by a demonized slave girl, who was very valuable to her heathen masters. When the slave girl continued for many days to annoy the apostles, Paul turned about and in the name of Jesus Christ commanded the evil spirit to come out of her. That very hour she was cured. "When her masters saw that the hope of their gains was gone, they caught Paul and Silas, and drew them into the market-place unto the rulers, and brought them to the magistrates." After a very hasty and riotous trial, Paul and Silas were condemned to be beaten. You understand, of course, what this meant. The back was made bare, the condemned person was bent forward till every muscle was strained to its severest tension, hands having been made secure to a post. Then two strong soldiers, sometimes with rods, sometimes with pieces of rope in which were intertwined pieces of metal or glass, scourged the condemned upon the back; blow after blow laying bare the flesh to the bone. Sometimes people died under the severity of the lashing. After a terrible beating, Paul and Silas were thrust into the inner prison, and their feet were made fast in the stocks. The inner prison was a dark, damp, dirty, dreary dungeon. The stocks, keeping the body in a fixed and uncomfortable position, added greatly to their trial. And then do you remember how Paul and Silas about midnight, some hours after the awful beating, when festering wounds and strained and tortured muscles were specially painful, began to complain bitterly of their hard trials, and of fate; of the wickedness and worthlessness of men, and of their pains? No! No! it does not read so in my Bible. "At midnight Paul and Silas prayed, and sang praises unto God." And they sang too so loudly and lustily that the prisoners heard them, and doubtless felt the power of such living. And now again Paul is a prisoner; and from his prison-house, he writes that wonderful song out of sorrow, the sweet love-letter to the Philippians. From this same prison-house, he writes to the Colossians of the sufficiency of Christ. From this same prison-house, he writes to the Ephesians in the words of the text, "And be not drunken with wine, wherein is riot, but be filled with the Spirit; speaking one to another in psalms and hymns and spiritual songs, singing and making melody with your heart to the Lord; giving thanks always for all things in the name of our Lord Jesus Christ to God, even the Father." Surely Paul has a right to be heard, when he speaks to us of the privilege and duty of gratitude.

And all down through the history of the Christian church, you will find examples of the truth that true prayer and true piety go hand in hand with praise. Indeed a complaining Christian is a paradox, a contradiction in terms. Theoretically and ideally this is true; yet in reality we find many professing Christians whose lives are filled with murmuring and complaining, with fussing and grumbling. Many seem to have forgotten Paul's injunction to the Philippians: "Do all things without murmurings and disputings; that ye may be blameless and harmless, children of God without blemish in the midst of a crooked and perverse generation, among whom ye are seen as luminaries, holding forth the word of life." It would be of great advantage both to the church and to the world if some Christians would move at once off from Grumble Street on to Thanksgiving Avenue. David said, "It is a good thing to give thanks unto the Lord." Let us think for a season of some reasons why we ought to cultivate the habit of gratitude:

1. We ought to cultivate the habit of gratitude because it is the proper thing to do. When we remember that "every good giving and every perfect boon is from above, coming down from the Father of lights, with whom can be no variation, neither shadow that is cast by turning"; when we recall how many and manifold mercies have been and are being continually showered upon us, undeserving of them as we are; we ought surely to recognize that gratitude felt and expressed is an eminently fitting and proper thing on our part. Though we were created in the image and likeness of God and made to rule, though man has a dignity and destiny nobler far than all other creatures, yet he is born into this world as one of the most helpless of all animals. The young of the lower animals somehow survive the most unfavorable conditions; but the baby man is so weak and so helpless that he is absolutely dependent upon parents or friends for the first few years of existence. When we become older and stronger we are apt to forget these things. We get proud. And yet, of what has such an inconsistent, weak, sinning one as man to be proud? Surely the recipient of so

many undeserved blessings ought to be thankful. In business lines or social walks, whenever we receive a favor, we acknowledge it by a receipt or a note of thanks. Should we not be as business-like and civil in respect to favors received from God? Common decency and courtesy would seem to demand it. Surely to receive a favor is to incur an obligation, and that obligation at the least is an obligation of gratitude. It was held by the Jews that "he who partakes of anything without giving thanks acts as if he were stealing it from God." If in the twilight of revelation the Jews recognized this truth, what shall be said of professed Christians who live kicking and complaining lives; Christians, so called, some of whom do not even have a blessing at the table? No true Jew ever omitted the table blessing. Jesus always gave thanks. Is it any wonder that Christ, when he had healed the ten lepers, and only one had returned to thank him for it, sadly asked, "Where are the nine?" "To be thankful" means really "to be thinkful," "to confess the facts," to acknowledge the truth. For decency's sake we ought to be grateful.

2. We ought to cultivate the habit of gratitude, because it is most pleasing to God. True parenthood in man must be more or less of a true shadow of parenthood in God. And that which pleases or displeases true earthly parents, must be analogous to what is pleasing or displeasing **to**

the Heavenly Parent. If this is so, let me ask you: O father; O mother; what is it in your child that is most pleasing, what most painful to you? In your life of devotion and self-sacrifice for those whom God has given you, does any sword cut with a keener blade, or thrust with more poignant steel, than the sword of ingratitude? Is anything more distressing in the home life than the presence of a thankless child? Does anything so wear upon the human heart as lack of true appreciation? Some years ago in the town of M——, in Ohio, I met a woman with a heavily burdened heart. She told me that her husband was paralyzed, and that she wished I might see him, and try to cheer him. At the time I was in a hospital and unable to get to him. He, however, could walk with one cane; and, as electric cars passed his door and mine, it was arranged that he was to call upon me. In a day or two he did so. During the first few minutes of our interview, he swore at almost everything imaginable, and in almost every way imaginable. When he had relieved himself in this fashion I asked him if he felt any better for it. I had tried almost everything for paralysis, but had never tried cursing. Perhaps he could recommend it as a helpful treatment. But no, with all of his swearing, he had not helped himself any, and could not recommend the habit. And then I asked him to tell me all about his paralysis. I saw that I could not reach him from the religious point of view, and thought I would try another plan. I induced him to tell me all about his condition, his ability and his disability; and when he had finished his story, I told mine. I did what I do not often do, I gave him every detail of a dark picture. I did not overdraw it. I told it just as it was. When I had finished my story, I thought Tom (for that was his name) would straighten up, cheer up, and say, "Well, if you can be cheerful, contented and grateful in such a condition, I can in my condition; for I can walk some and get about, but you must be carried." It was my earnest hope that Tom would make such a resolve, and that our visit would be of permanent benefit; but, alas, I didn't know Tom. When I had finished my story, instead of cheering up and bracing up, Tom knitted his brow and said: "Ugh! That's tough! I suppose I'll be that way some day!" Now what could one do to cheer such a person as that, a person who would always look upon the dark side of things? A person who would not only continually complain of present trials, but would spend the time in anticipating possible worse ones? Some days afterwards I saw again Tom's wife, and I said to her, "My dear woman, what is it in your life that is continually wearing upon you, that whitens your hair and writes wrinkles on your brow? What is it that is breaking your health so? Is it because Tom is paralyzed? Is it because you have so much hard work to do?" "Oh," she said, "it isn't because Tom is paralyzed. It isn't because of the work. When I married Tom he was well and strong. Everything was bright and fair. But I married him for weal or woe, for better or worse. It isn't because Tom is paralyzed. It isn't because of the work. I love him. I loved him when he was strong and well. I love him none the less now. It's a pleasure to wait upon him and help him. Don't you know what a woman means when she says 'I love him'? Ah, no, it isn't because Tom's paralyzed. But Tom don't do as he once did. He was once so grateful and appreciative. He seems now to take for granted everything I do for him. He seems to forget to say 'Thank you.'" "But," said I, "Tom told me only a few days ago that he had the best wife in town." "Ah," she said—and I can see now the trembling of her form, the twitching of the muscles of the face, and the tears chasing each other down her cheeks —"he hasn't told me that for a long time; not for a long time." And when I saw Tom I told him how his wife was starving for gratitude.

And I want to say to you, O husband: what your wife needs to cheer her heart and make glad her home and yours, is not electric lights, not a new dress, or a new bonnet, so much as it is for you to be as gallant and grateful and appreciative of her, as you were when you were a young lover, or were in the first years of wedded life. Grateful appreciation will do more to make her step light, to keep her face bright and her heart full of sunshine and cheer than almost any other one thing. And, O wife: to you, too, a similar message comes. Nothing will do more to cheer and inspire and brace a hard working and heavily burdened husband than the sweet appreciation, felt and expressed, of a true, grateful wife. And here also I see before me many bright boys and girls who are beloved by parents and who indeed love their parents. But, boys and girls, sometimes you forget. Who is it that provides the beautiful ribbons and bright dresses, the balls and bats, the school-books, pencils and papers, etc.? Why, when I was a boy, we used an old broken piece of a slate; and with a rag and in an unmentionable way we cleaned our broken slates. But the doctors have said that rags and sponges and slates must go, and now you have pencils and paper and tablets; and every few weeks you must have new books. Boys and girls!

> "You are the heirs of all the ages
> In the foremost files of Time."

You have almost everything. But, under God, to whom are you indebted for all of these blessings? Generally to a hard working, faithful father, or a self-sacrificing, patient mother, or to both. And, boys and girls, nothing will so please your father and mother as your gratitude expressed in obedient and faithful lives, and in words of love and thankfulness. When we go from here to our homes, let us all turn over a new leaf, and begin to cultivate the habit of more freely expressing our gratitude. Now, if this is pleasing in human relationships, it is most surely well-pleasing to God. One of the awful charges brought against the heathen world, in that remarkable first chapter of Romans, is that "knowing God, they glorified him not as God, neither gave thanks." God, I believe, hungers for, and delights in the expressed gratitude of his creatures.

3. We ought to cultivate a thankful spirit, because it will produce in us humility and industry. One of the things which God hates is pride. In all parts of Scripture it receives the severest condemnation. On the other hand God is said to have two thrones, one in the heights of heaven, the other in the humble heart: for Isaiah says, "Thus saith the high and lofty One that inhabiteth eternity, whose name is Holy: I dwell in the high and holy place, with him also that is of a contrite and humble spirit." And the psalmist says, "The Lord is nigh unto them that are of a broken heart, and saveth such as be of a contrite spirit." And again, "The sacrifices of God are a broken spirit: a broken and contrite heart, O God, thou wilt not despise." And both James and Peter tell us, "God resisteth the proud, but giveth grace

to the humble." Jesus, too, the only time he ever defined his heart-life, said, "For I am meek and lowly in heart." If we desire, then, to cultivate and acquire more of this desirable humility, let us cultivate the spirit of gratitude, for gratitude and humility go hand in hand. A really proud person is seldom grateful. A truly grateful person generally has a humble heart. He, who forms the habit of constantly bearing in mind the manifold blessings and mercies showered upon him, feels more and more his own unworthiness, and comes more and more into the spirit of true humility. But the spirit of gratitude will not only produce in us humility, but will also incite us to industry. As we think of our many reasons for gratitude, and of our unworthiness to receive one-half that we enjoy, we shall find ourselves spurred on to honest toil and earnest endeavor, that we may in some way show our appreciation and become more worthy of our blessings. Thus will the habit of gratitude produce in us the two conditions of true success, humility and industry. I am told that over the gates leading from one quadrangle to another in a great English university is this significant inscription. Over the first gate is written "Per humilitatem;" over the second gate "Per honestatem;" over the third gate "Ad honorem." "Through humility, through industry (or integrity) to honor." These are the two gates to true honor and success in every walk in life; and if we shall cultivate the spirit of gratitude, we shall not find it hard either to be humble or industrious.

4. The habit of thankfulness will develop and enlarge any one. Ingratitude belittles, warps and dwarfs anybody, while the spirit of gratitude makes for manhood and womanhood. "The real size of a gentleman or lady," some one has said, "can easily be determined by the amount of their appreciation of others, and of favors received." In other words lack of gratitude is lack of manhood and womanhood. No one is smaller than the ingrate and the miser. Gratitude enlarges and develops.

5. The spirit of gratitude makes life easier and more enjoyable. Real gratitude for anything increases the enjoyment of it, and the expression of such gratitude increases both the gratitude and the enjoyment. After my wheel-chair has been used for a few days, it begins to creak and squeak, and I know that it needs oil. And I come into touch with many people who are full of creaks and squeaks, and who need some oil, or other lubricating fluid, to remove the whining of the wheels. I know of no oil like the oil of gladness. "He that hath a merry heart hath a continual feast." And the person who cultivates at all times the thankful spirit has found a lubricating oil, which will remove much of the wear and tear, much of the jar and jostle in the ma-

chinery of life. It will refresh body, mind and spirit.

6. And again, the thankful spirit helps others and wins friendship. "A merry heart doeth good like medicine." And he who cultivates a thankful spirit always has friends. Everybody likes flowers. He who always scatters sunshine is always a favorite. You don't care to see the person who goes about with a doleful face, and a dismal whine, and always talks of his miseries and woes, and sees nothing but dark shadows and cypress trees. Some people seem to enjoy their miseries, and only approach some shadow of a shade of a shining when they have some one's ears into which, with unfeigned contentment, they can pour their oft-repeated tale of woe. But such people generally have few friends, and never are popular with any one. Side by side with these who spend their days in overhauling their personal miseries, are the howling pessimists, who see no cause for gratitude anywhere. Some commiseration is to be felt for those who, overcome by their personal trials and woes, have gotten into the unpleasant and unprofitable business of taking frequent inventories of their miseries. But for those kickers who deliberately put on a pair of the bluest spectacles in order to see everything in the darkest and most discouraging light, nothing but the severest condemnation is fitting. In such black darkness, no good thrives. These, then,

are some of the reasons why we ought to be grateful. It is the proper thing to do; it is most pleasing to God; it tends to produce humility and industry; it develops and enlarges one; it makes life easier and more enjoyable; it makes for friendship and helpfulness.

Praise is one of the greatest acts of which we are capable. Heaven is filled with praise. Thanksgiving constitutes the very atmosphere of the kingdom. Everybody's life ought to be musical. God intended that every life should be so. God's world, as He made it, and wherever sin has not destroyed its melody, is vocal with music. There is the carol of the bird, the ripple of the brook, the soft zephyrs of the evening; even the busy bee hums a merry tune. Man alone withholds his note of praise. Yet everybody has a capacity for praise, for music. Only demons hate harmony. They alone love discord, and make it their business to produce as much of it as possible everywhere. Surely Christians, redeemed by the precious blood of Christ, and saved from the penalty and dominion of sin, ought to have musical lives. Such surely ought to be "filled with the Spirit, speaking one to another in psalms and hymns and spiritual songs, singing and making melody with the heart to the Lord; giving thanks always for all things, in the name of our Lord Jesus Christ to God, even the Father." Christianity is particularly a religion of joy and thankfulness. We must so live it if we are to be Christ's representatives and be true witnesses of His kingdom. He desired that His joy might remain in His disciples, and that their joy might be full. We must realize His spirit of joy and thankfulness in our own lives, if our living is to be of much inspiration to ourselves, or of much helpfulness and attractiveness unto others. Some one has truly written:

> "A religion without thanksgiving, praise and joy
> Is like a flower without perfume, tint or honey;
> There may be such a flower, but surely
> No one would care to pluck it."

If your religion is "a religion without thanksgiving, praise or joy," I don't want it. I wouldn't have it. I should be surprised to find anybody who would want it.

But you say that it is easy to be thankful for some things, but impossible always to be thankful for all things. Any heathen could be thankful for some things. This is not a Christian grace. The Christian grace is to obey Paul's injunction and give "thanks always for all things in the name of our Lord Jesus Christ unto God, even the Father." "In the name of our Lord Jesus Christ" and "unto God, even the Father," in these two thoughts is the key to "giving thanks always for all things." Christ being my Savior, and God being my Father, make it possible for me to sing:

> "Father, for gain or loss I owe
> Thee song and prayer. How do I know
> With these dim-sighted eyes?
> Grief may be good in dark disguise."

For the Christian, gratitude and thankfulness are not and must not be dependent upon outward conditions and circumstances. They must rest upon the settled conviction of the soul that the Father's love and the Savior's grace will, if you are willing and obedient, make "all things to work together for good." God, my Father, is supremely interested in my welfare. Whatever touches my life, therefore, comes by His permitting or providing providence through the circle of his enspering love. I need not know just what the immediate or the remote outcome is to be. I don't need to know. He knows.

> "I do not ask that God should always make my pathway bright.
> I only pray that he will hold my hand throughout the night."

At first when the blow falls, manlike I may stagger and cry out with the human Savior, "O Father, if it be possible, let this cup pass." Yet He knows how human I am. He knows what is in man. He will be patient and compassionate, and wait till I learn to say: "Nevertheless, not my will, but Thine be done." Even in sorrow and for sorrow I may learn to be thankful: as I note the sweetening and strengthening of char

THANKFULNESS

acter and the disciplinary effect of trial upon me; as I note how it drives me closer to Christ, helps me to realize my need, opens up and makes real to me the sympathy and friendship of Jesus, and the sweetness and richness of the manifold promises; as I note how it so humanizes me and teaches me to sympathize with and help others. Yes, even in sorrow and for sorrow I may be grateful. God helping me so to do, I will learn at all times and for all things to give thanks. (1) I will look at the bright side of a dark subject. I will look away to the light, and the shadow will be behind me. I do not destroy the shadow, nor deny its existence. I prefer to look at the light, and the shadow falls into the background. This is both scientific and Christian. "The sweetest songs of the nightingale are only warbled in darkness, and the clearest notes of thankfulness and joy are only heard in the midnight of affliction." (2) I will not only magnify my mercies and take frequent inventory of my blessings; but I will keep down my extravagances, and learn with a few necessary things therewith to be content. Jealousy and covetousness shall not dwell in my heart. (3) I will keep usefully busy and spend my life in helpfulness. And (4) I will learn to live a life of trust, one day at a time; lest I may not be grateful, and may miss present opportunities for service, and present blessings, by worrying over imaginary or future ills. In these four ways I will learn to be "thankful always for all things in the name of our Lord Jesus Christ to God, even the Father." Can you say it? Will you will to do it from now on? Then you may learn to sing "songs in the night," even as Fanny Crosby did, in her more than forty years of blindness. For when she was only eight years old, and had lost her sight for life, she said:

> "Oh, what a happy soul am I!
> Although I cannot see,
> I am resolved that in this world
> Contented I will be.
> How many blessings I enjoy
> That other people don't!
> To weep and sigh, because I'm blind,
> I cannot, and I won't."

Or, with another of God's nightingales, an invalid for life and bereft in the very morning of womanhood of her heart's earthly king; with Mrs. Steele, another author of many songs of the night, you too may learn to sing:

> "Father, whate'er of earthly bliss
> Thy sovereign will denies,
> Accepted at thy throne of grace,
> Let this petition rise:
> Give me a calm and thankful heart,
> From every murmur free,
> The blessings of thy love impart
> And help me live to thee."

www.ingramcontent.com/pod-product-compliance
Lightning Source LLC
Chambersburg PA
CBHW021838230426
43669CB00008B/1003